IMAGES OF

Guildford

Front endpaper: A panorama of Guildford from the Warwick's Bench area taken in late Victorian times. The chimney of Lascelles Tickner & Co's Castle Brewery can be seen on the left. St Nicolas Church and the town mill stand out in the middle of the picture, while to the right and slightly further in the distance three gas-holders can be seen.

Back endpaper: Lines in the sand: This 1970 photograph is so revealing and important because in many ways it marks the end of one era in Guildford and the start of the next. In the foreground, there is clear evidence of preparatory work being carried out on the site of what was to become the new £10 million Royal Surrey County Hospital, first mooted in 1963, opened on 2 January 1980, and dedicated by the Queen in the following year. Immediately beyond the hospital site is Bannisters Field with its football pitch, athletics track and cricket ground. In 1989, the borough council sold 7.2 acres of this amenity to Tesco, which built Guildford's second out-of-town superstore, and then used the £28 million receipts to fund the building of the hotly-contested but now highly popular Spectrum Leisure Centre on the north side of Stoke Park.

IMAGES OF

Surrey Advertiser

Guildford

by Graham Collyer
and David Rose

The Breedon Books
Publishing Company
Derby

First published in Great Britain by
The Breedon Books Publishing Company Limited
Breedon House, 44 Friar Gate, Derby, DE1 1DA.
1998

ISBN 1 85983 120 6

Printed and bound by Butler & Tanner Ltd., Selwood Printing Works, Caxton
Road, Frome, Somerset.

Colour separations by Freelance Repro, Leicester.

Jackets printed by Lawrence-Allen, Avon.

Contents

Introduction

IN selecting nearly 400 pictures for *Images of Guildford* we have been fortunate to have been allowed access to a number of wonderful collections held by private individuals and public organisations.

For many of the views throughout the book we thank Graham Richardson and Tim and Jackie Winter for their picture postcards. John Janaway and the staff of the Surrey Local Studies Library have provided many pictures and useful information – along with Mary Mackey, Laurence Spring and the staff of the Guildford Muniment Room, who allowed us to copy photographs from the huge collection of material relating to Dennis Bros and Drummond's. These two essential sources of information for local historians have now been transferred and amalgamated at the new Surrey History Centre in Woking.

The librarian at the Guildford Institute, Clare Miles, found us two superb scrapbooks full of old photographs of the town centre, including many of shop fronts taken in 1922.

Peter and Stuart Phillips have for a long time been collecting pictures, memorabilia and collating statistics on Guildford's two former football clubs – the Pinks and the City. Their pictures and information have been most valuable.

Architectural historian Charles Brooking loaned us many photographs of buildings taken just before they were demolished at the end of the 1960s and early 1970s, and these form the basis of the chapter *Lost Guildford*.

John and Christopher Hodgson, father and son, of the long established firm of chartered architects and interior designers Hodgson, Lunn and Co, provided us with useful pictures of buildings their practice has designed, such as the Picture Palace, not to mention some

rare photographs of Guildford City FC, of which John's father, Frederick, was such an integral part for 50 years.

The majority of the views in the chapter about the cathedral are from its own archives and we thank Eric and Shirley Mills for their assistance.

The Wey Navigation at its headquarters at Dapdune Wharf has a tremendous collection of pictures (all stored and available to view on computer) and we thank Alison Dingle and her staff for their help.

A number of the photographs used in the *War, Military and Remembrance* chapter are from the collection held at the Queen's Royal Surrey Regiment Museum at Clandon Park, looked after by Colonel Peter Durrant, Penny James and staff. Pageant master David Clarke supplied us with some lovely images of the many productions with which he has been involved.

Co-author David Rose provided many picture postcards plus contemporary illustrations of some of the antique bottles in his own collection and those from fellow Surrey Bottle Collectors' Club members Clive Wicks, Geoff Killick and Terry Simmonds.

Many photographs were discovered in the *Surrey Advertiser's* own files. Stored away for many years, fantastic rare views literally kept falling out from drawers as we delved further into our own huge collection.

We have also used several dozen photographs from the collection of the late Eric Tyrrell, a Guildford architect and surveyor, which was donated to us. These scenes were mostly taken during the 1960s before many changes were made to the town centre.

We are grateful to the following people who also contributed pictures: Richard Ford, Chris

Roberts, Douglas Barnes, Darren Burge, Sandra Young and The Wilky Group, Peter Slade of the Guildford Society, Ken Sutcliffe, Ben Green and Geoff Strickland of Guildford Golf Club, Roger Nicklin, Chris Nixon, Peter Pallot, Bernard Parke, Margaret Jack of Guildford Chamber of Commerce, Peter Sherwood, who has taken numerous aerial photographs of the town, Mike Fisher, Donald Stevens, Leslie and Marion Smailes, and Hilda Weekes.

Thanks must also go to the curator of Guildford Museum, Matthew Alexander, George Titus, of Fotolab Express, and Dennis Specialist Vehicles.

Valuable work in helping to prepare this book was undertaken by the following colleagues: Photographers Terry Habgood and Steve Porter, our secretaries, Diana Piercy and Rebecca Kingshott, Karen Henderson, Ray Stewart, Rodney Smithers and the late Arthur Gaines, who died while this book was being completed. We must also thank our wives, Ann and Helen, for their assistance in reading proofs and offering sound advice.

Again we thank everyone who contributed in one way or another.

We are proud that there is a wealth of historic images of Guildford kept in safe hands for posterity. We believe that the selection reproduced here is probably just the tip of an iceberg and many more pictures are waiting to be discovered.

Graham Collyer and David Rose
Summer, 1998.

Around the Town

Welcome to Guildford: One of the first things Edwardian travellers would notice when entering via the town bridge was a mass of advertising from firms including jewellers Spikins from Dent, T.Andrews' music shop, George Welburn tailors, and Emery & Son auctioneers.

A quite different view of the River Wey looking up towards the High Street. Here is the version of the town bridge which dated from 1824. It suffered substantial damage from floodwater and debris from Moon's timber yard on 15 February 1900, after the river burst its banks. It was replaced by a new bridge in 1902. Note the small brick-built arch and the iron railings.

When postcard publisher Percy Lloyd took this photograph at about the turn of the century you could stand in the middle of Quarry Street without fear of being run over. How things have changed today. There is a wonderful collection of paraphernalia hanging up outside Angell & Son's store. Trunks and cases can be seen projecting from the first-floor windows.

There has probably been a Guildhall in the High Street since medieval times. Today's Guildhall dates from about 1550. The frontage was added in 1683 along with the case of the famous clock, the mechanism being much older. It is believed that it was a gift to the town from John Aylward who was seeking the freedom to set up in business here. Notice that the face of the clock looks different from today. During the nineteenth century the original dial was replaced by a glass one illuminated by gas lights. The original parts were reinstated in 1898, despite nearly being thrown away a few years earlier.

Market Street from the High Street with the Bull's Head, one of Guildford's fondly remembered pubs, on the right. Timothy White's Cash Chemists is on the left on the site once occupied by the Red Lion Hotel.

A classic early Edwardian view looking down Guildford High Street. On the left can be seen the main entrances to the White Hart Hotel, also known as The County Hotel, seen here in its closing years. It is believed that there had been an hotel on the site since at least the middle of the sixteenth century. The Bonner family ran it for most of the nineteenth century and finally sold up in 1904. It was soon demolished and Guildford's first Sainsbury's was built in its place.

In 1934 pupils from the Central School in Sydenham Road were given a Box Brownie camera and told to go and take pictures of their choice. What they recorded is a fascinating insight into everyday life. Here we see Timothy White's store in the High Street on the corner of Market Street, with G.C.Bateman opticians next door.

The Hospital of the Blessed Trinity, better known as Abbot's Hospital, is, without doubt, one of Guildford's most beautiful buildings. Completed in 1622, it was Archbishop George Abbot's gift in the form of an almshouse to his home town. Twenty old Guildfordians resided there when it opened. In recent years it has been extended and continues to provide accommodation for the elderly.

This small cottage was Archbishop George Abbot's birthplace and was situated just over the town bridge in the yard of Crooke's brewery. Today, the George Abbot pub, formerly the Greyhound, stands near the site of these buildings. Note the water pump, wooden barrel and stoneware jars.

This view existed only for a few years after the buildings which made up Ram Corner were pulled down to ease the movement of traffic at the junction of the High Street and Chertsey Street. Bank chambers in the neo-Georgian style rose from the piece of land seen here on the left-hand side.

A view of the upper High Street at about the time of World War One. The Royal Grammar School building looks drab by comparison to its bright whitewashed façade of today. To the right is the photographic studio of Mrs Reid FRPS, now occupied by Nicklins opticians.

The upper High Street in the 1920s. The left-hand side has changed considerably with today's shops situated much further back from the road. The tree in the distance is the same one seen in the picture below.

Unrecognisable today is this scene where the upper High Street divides off into London Road, left, and Epsom Road. A pair of iron gates leads to Poyle House. The site, running along the sides of both roads, was developed into shops and offices in the 1930s, just before the nearby Odeon cinema was built.

If you have time when sitting at the traffic lights at the junction of Epsom Road with Waterden and Warren Roads today, you will notice the following changes from this 1900s view. The porch, supported by a pair of columns, adjoining the Sanford Arms, is long gone. So is the gas lamp just behind the little girl in the foreground. Some may recall the monkey puzzle tree which stood in the garden of the house in Epsom Road opposite the pub. Here it is no more than twenty feet high. The stone setts around the drains and by the kerb stones have long been covered up. The Sanford Arms Inn was built in the 1860s and named after a family which was related to its owner, Hodgsons Kingston Brewery. In this picture the name above the door is F.G.Eaton, presumably the licensee. However, one of the authors has a small glass whisky bottle dating from the same period etched with the words A.E.Puttock, Sanford Arms, Guildford.

Friary, Holroyd & Healy's brewery can be seen in the middle of this view looking along Bridge Street in about 1910. The business flourished under the guidance of its owners, the Masters family, throughout the late nineteenth century, with the firm buying up various other smaller breweries in Surrey. Further breweries in Sussex and Hampshire were absorbed in the twentieth century. In 1963 Allied Breweries took over the then named Friary Meux company and brewing itself ceased in Guildford in 1969.

It is always the children who stop to look at the photographer at work. A busy scene at Guildford cattle market in Woodbridge Road. The market moved there from North Street in 1895. The police station and law courts now stand on this site.

The Prince of Wales public house in Woodbridge Road, with St Saviour's Church in the background, was designed by Henry Peak and constructed in 1893 for the Cobham United Brewery. In its later years it was a Watney's house and was pulled down in 1972.

Compare this view of Haydon Place to what you can see today and you will notice a number of changes. The houses on the left no longer stand, nor does the building on the right which was for many years used by the Guildford Co-operative Society. In the early 1980s it was used as an indoor market which, for a while, proved quite popular. The building standing on the corner of Martyr Road (centre right) is now the Guildford Antique Centre. At one time it was occupied by P.Norman Button, photographers and picture framers.

North Street with the market in full swing and all the stalls openly displaying their goods. Note that in the days before the motor car the stalls faced out into the road. Many of the buildings survive to this day, but not the one on the extreme right.

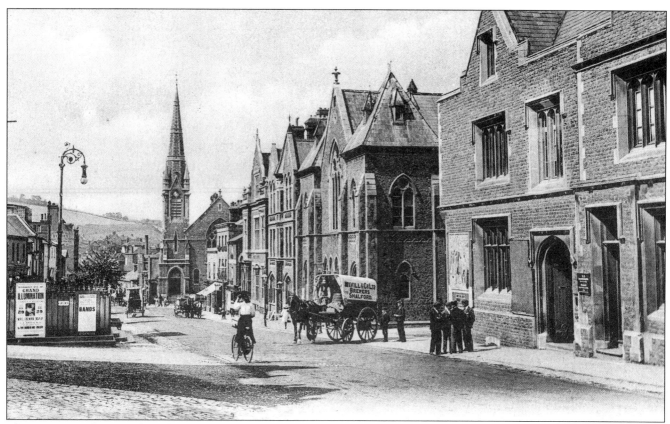

The County and Borough Halls, Congregational Chapel and the Methodist Church with its steeple dominate this view of North Street. Note the fancy lamppost and underground lavatories with their smart iron railings.

Market Street viewed from North Street is heavily decorated for an event that could possibly be the coronation of George V in June 1911. The offices and printing works of the *Surrey Advertiser* were about halfway up on the left-hand side.

The top of North Street looking towards Chertsey Street at about the turn of the century. The large advertising posters are near to where the entrance of Cinderella's nightclub is today.

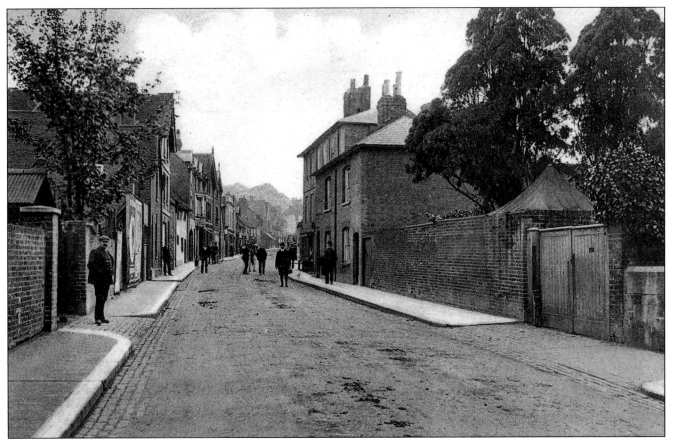

The gates and the brick wall on the right have disappeared, but this part of Chertsey Street looks very much the same today as it did some 80 years ago.

Central Buildings, built in 1924, with its attractive concrete pillars was once the home of Gates Stores on the ground floor, with the Automobile Association occupying the upper floors. The firm of Cow & Gate had moved around the corner from its old High Street premises to this one in North Street.

A superb turn of the century picture postcard view looking down Chapel Street from Castle Street. The shopfronts may have changed but the buildings themselves remain largely unaltered.

Three young boys 'caught' by the Edwardian cameraman. What they were doing in Castle Arch we will never know. The picture is neatly framed by the ancient arch which is thought to have been built in 1256 by John of Gloucester, the master mason to Henry III.

The fish ponds in the Castle Grounds, seen here during the Edwardian era, were considerably larger than they are today.

A view of the Castle Keep and Grounds taken a few years after it was opened to the public by the corporation in 1888. The stone Keep dates from 1125 and has had a chequered history. Owned by a succession of English kings, it was still occupied in the early 1600s, but its then owner, Francis Carter, soon gave up and moved to a new home nearby. When the plans for the pleasure gardens were being drawn up in the 1880s, one scheme was to demolish the Keep. Thankfully, the authorities saw better sense!

The Rev Charles Lutwidge Dodgson, better known as the author Lewis Carroll, leased The Chestnuts in Castle Hill in 1868. It was the home of Dodgson's six unmarried sisters until the early years of this century. Although he lived in Oxford, he stayed at The Chestnuts during holiday periods. He died in Guildford on 14 January 1898, and is buried in the cemetery on The Mount.

This Jolly Farmer public house in Shalford Road dates from 1913. The cottages beyond have long since made way for road widening and the Millbrook car park.

A sleepy view of Denzil Road at the time of World War One with the only vehicle being a dustcart. This picture postcard was sent from number 58. The writer, presumably a serviceman, indicated his billet by marking a tiny cross above the window of the shop on the left.

Agraria Road, with the unfinished cathedral in the background, as you may never have seen it before. Today, it is always full of parked vehicles which makes it difficult for traffic to manoeuvre between Madrid Road and Farnham Road, a popular cut-through for motorists seeking to avoid the one-way system in the town centre.

From the top of St Catherine's Hill down to Artington, Booker's Tower can just be seen on the horizon. Charles Booker, a former Mayor of Guildford, lost two sons, both at the age of 15. He had the 70ft high tower built in their memory. Large detached houses in Guildown stand out in this view of about 100 years ago. The entrance to Braboeuf Manor, now the College of Law, can be seen in the bottom left of the picture.

A turn of the century view of Guildford seen from about halfway up The Mount. Four of the town's churches can be seen – St Nicolas, St Mary's and Holy Trinity to the right of the picture while, almost on the horizon to the far left, St Saviour's before its steeple had been built.

Industry & Commerce

Frank Lasham, chairman of Guildford Chamber of Trade in 1908, was also a printer in the town, and he designed an attractive cover for the menu of the organisation's fourth annual dinner held in the Lion Hotel on 29 January.

Frank Lasham's artistry was probably also behind this souvenir, so typical of the period. The reception marked Shopping Week in Guildford, an event organised by the Chamber of Trade with the aim of getting people into the town centre in order to boost the coffers of the business community.

The mineral water firm of Shelvey & Co Ltd had branches in Brighton, Eastbourne and Worthing. In 1905 it opened a manufactory in Guildford on the corner of Onslow Street and Bedford Road. Its manager was Edgar Purnell who took over the business in his own name in 1918. Here are three of its Guildford delivery men. The fellow in the middle is still wearing his cycle clips. Did he arrive late for the photograph or was he hoping to nip off quickly?

There is nothing like showing off your wares to help generate sales. Tom Picken's Stores was at the bottom of North Street where the Friary Centre is today.

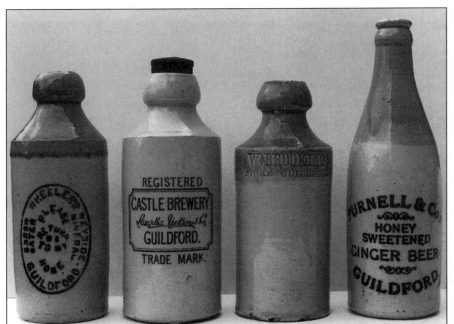

Around 100 years ago local firms had their own bottles, pots and jars in which to package their products. Although these items have been buried in rubbish tips for many years, they continue to be dug out of the ground and cleaned up by enthusiastic collectors. Some rare and highly desirable examples, now regarded as antiques in their own right, have been known to change hands for considerable amounts of money. Pictured above left are four stoneware ginger beer bottles used by Guildford mineral water manufacturers from the 1880s to the 1930s. Right is a stoneware hot water bottle marked with the name of Tom Picken's Stores, Guildford, and an advertising item for the same firm in the form of a matchstriker.

The firm of Gates can be traced back to 1771 as a grocery business in the High Street. By 1881, it was boasting that it stocked beers, wines and spirits from no fewer than 40 brewers. At about this time, Charles Gates handed over the business to his two sons, Leonard, and Charles Arthur. They soon decided to do away with the alcoholic side and to prove their point it is said they hauled all the remaining stock up from their cellars and tipped it into the gutters of the High Street. They then sold cream, buying the milk from local farms. The firm was trading under the name of The West Surrey Central Dairy Company and its original trademark was a pair of wrought-iron gates. A new emblem was devised in 1891 after the brothers had juggled with pictures of cows and gates cut out of paper. Soon the words Cow & Gate began appearing on the firm's literature and advertisements, and over the next 50 years the name went around the world as the firm grew. This is a turn of the century view of the shop front in the High Street, which was next to the Three Pigeons public house.

An advertisement for The West Surrey Central Dairy Company containing the all-important slogan, 'Babies Love It'. The name Cow & Gate Ltd was adopted in 1929 and export trade during the 1930s reached all corners of the world. One story recalls two cases of baby food sent to India at the urgent request of an un-named maharajah. It was only later that the firm learned that the food was bought for use in his racing stables! Another memorable advertising slogan was 'The Food of Royal Babies'. Although the name lives on today, Cow & Gate Ltd merged with United Dairies in 1959 to become Unigate.

MOTHERS, NOTE.

The Safe Milk for the Hot Months

IS THE

COW and GATE

Germ-free   Digestible

DRIED MILK.

In Summer and at all Seasons, Babies thrive on this COMPLETE FOOD, which is the most PERFECT SUBSTITUTE FOR MOTHER'S MILK.

Highly Approved by the Medical Profession.

BABIES LOVE IT.

Free Samples and Literature, apply to Sole Manufacturers—

The West Surrey Central Dairy Co., LIMITED,

GUILDFORD. Surrey.

Another striking advertisement for The West Surrey Central Dairy Company.

The staff of Guildford tailor Bernard Weatherill outside its Bridge Street premises. Note the lettering in the right-hand window advertising that motor clothing was then a speciality. This was the era when sitting behind the wheel of a new-fangled motor car was still regarded as something of a sport.

As the signwriting on the vehicles confirms, J.W.Bentley was a wholesale grocer based in the High Street. It also sold beer and ale in black glass cork-stoppered bottles. The reason why this Edwardian era photograph was taken is unknown; the group could be members of staff and their families.

The Guildford Picture Framing & Moulding Company, owned by Tom Pallot, was situated at 1a Commercial Road, roughly where the main entrance to the Friary Centre is today. Mr Pallot was one of the first residents of Onslow Village in the early 1920s.

Boxes galore of Rowntrees Cocoa, Kemp's Biscuits and Mansion Polish: An interior shot of Stephenson's Wholesale Grocers a few months before it moved from the High Street to Castle Street in June 1925. Thomas Stephenson, who was mayor in 1888, had taken over the business from John Crooke in the early 1880s.

Lascelles Tickner & Co's Castle Brewery in Portsmouth Road was second in size to Guildford's Friary Brewery. As well as brewing beer it also produced a wide range of mineral waters. This is a patent Codd bottle with a glass marble trapped in its neck. When filled with fizzy pop the marble was forced against a rubber ring at the top of the neck forming a water- and air-tight seal. Between the 1880s and about the end of World War One, the firm used thousands of Codd bottles. This example, however, is most rare, due to its 'dumpy' shape and amber coloured glass, as opposed to the common aqua glass varieties.

White's Farm in Warren Road sold its own cream in these delightful 3in high stoneware churn-shaped pots.

At one time Guildford had up to a dozen local dairies supplying it with milk and related products. It was not until after World War One that milk was commonly sold in glass bottles. Examples from the 1920s and 1930s, like this half-pint from Burden's Grange Farm Dairy, in Stoughton, can be recognised by their wide mouths. The milk was sealed in by a cardboard disc.

31

Fred Bailey was a well-known tobacconist and confectioner in Guildford up until World War Two, and his van prominently advertised his business to residents in the town and rural areas.

A traction engine has just drawn a rather large load on to the weighbridge which once stood at the bottom of North Street. Everyone around has tried to get in the picture. The load had possibly just arrived by rail as lettering on the wagon reveals that the hauliers were agents to the London & South Western Railway.

Only the most inquisitive of local historians can hope to find clues of Guildford's brickmaking industry. There are few records apart from the scars of clay pits marked on nineteenth century maps and the names of brick and tile manufacturers listed in old town directories. This view, taken in Guildford Park Road, shows a traction engine and trailer of T.Mitchell who had a large brickworks in this part of the town. Its chimney can be seen between the two houses and the works survived long enough to provide bricks for the cathedral. An abundance of clay in Rydes Hill, Stoughton and Worplesdon provided the raw material for other manufacturers. In the mid-nineteenth century there was a brickworks at Pitch Place owned by a W.Henley. William Wells was making bricks in Rydes Hill in 1867. By 1882 he had been replaced by Charles Mitchell, and in Stoughton there was Frederick Berry. As the late nineteenth century building boom in the town took place other manufacturers set up locally, including Alfred Bonner, Dathan Dickinson, Robert Earwacker, William Smith, George Lowe and Faggeter. A house with the name of Brickworks Cottage in Keens Lane, Rydes Hill, is a modern-day reminder of this once important Guildford industry. The kilns in Keens Lane were abandoned at about the time of World War One.

Arthur Drummond was born in 1871 and lived at Pinks Hill near Wood Street. Like his father, he was a talented artist and had exhibited at the Royal Academy by the the age of 19. He was also interested in model engineering, and in 1896 designed and built his own lathe. With the help of his brother, Frank, an engineer, he set up production in a workshop adjacent to their home, Old Gables. In 1902 they opened a factory at Broadstreet, seen here from an aerial view looking north.

This is thought to be the original Drummond lathe. Soon the firm offered a number of different designs and within a few years they were being exported around the world. During World War One, Drummond's made lathes for the Royal Navy.

Drummond's range of machine tools was expanded again after World War One. The Broad Street factory was then employing about 300 people. Although times were hard in many parts of Britain, Drummond's as well as other Guildford factories, such as Dennis Bros, had enough orders to be able to increase its workforce. Employees moved to the town from many parts of the country. This is a 1960s view of the factory and offices.

During World War Two Drummond's again produced vital equipment for the war effort in the form of multi-tool lathes and gear shapers. Standard lathe production continued in the 1950s and 1960s and seen here is a later variation of the firm's Maxicut lathe. By the 1970s the business was in decline. As part of Staveley Machine Tools Ltd, it finally closed in 1981 and the site was turned into a small business and industrial park.

James Angel, seated left, with his family, came to Guildford in 1889 from Pembroke Dock in Wales and started an ironmongery business.

Seen here as Angel, Son & Gray Ltd, in 1926, the business which was now selling all types of building materials and supplies became something of a landmark in Commercial Road near the corner of Onslow Street and Woodbridge Road.

The firm also occupied premises on the opposite side of Woodbridge Road, too. Although this building remains, you would not stand a chance of parking a car here today.

A 1959 view of Angel's where today buses leave the Friary Centre in Commercial Road. Note the St Saviour's Church Hall building with its high pitched roof. It was soon to be demolished to make way for more expansion by Angel's.

The trade counter at Angel's in the late 1950s.

Staff demonstrate how the latest Hoover vacuum cleaner works in the electrical appliances department at Angel's in the 1950s.

Just into the 1960s and the new Angel's building is taking shape in this view looking up Onslow Street towards St Saviour's Church.

Angel's Corner, as it became known, showing the company's modern showrooms of 7,000 sq ft. The large Number 1 Onslow Street building occupies this site today. When the Friary development took place, Angels of Guildford moved to Mary Road. The company was taken over by the Wilky Group in 1982.

Sutton & Co's shop in the upper High Street is promoting 'the up to date cycle' in this 1922 view. To the left is the premises of coach-builders May & Jacobs which was established in 1800 by a Mr W.Watson. The town's municipal offices were built on this site. They were pulled down in 1987 to be replaced by shops and offices.

J.Hepworth & Son Ltd has its window full of hats and fashions for men, women and children. Above, in this 1920s view are the offices of the *Guildford and Godalming Weekly Press*. This newspaper was owned by Biddles and was printed at its works in Martyr Road.

Williams Bros for many years was the town's principal newspaper and magazine wholesaler. This is a view of its Onslow Street shop.

Some of these upper High Street buildings can still be seen today although the business of Crow Bros and Elaine have long gone. The estate agents and auctioneers, Clarke Gammon, are still in business, now located further down the High Street with auction rooms in Bedford Road.

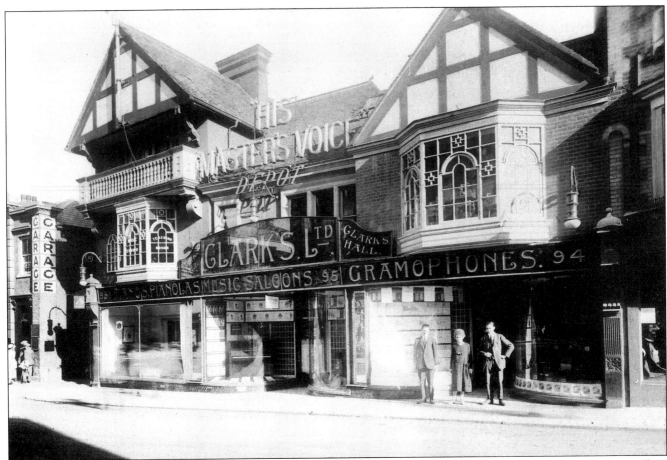

At the bottom of the High Street, below the junction with Quarry Street, was the grand façade of Clark's music shop selling everything from pianolas to gramophones.

A little further up the High Street was Jackson's Motor Works and G.Oliver & Sons Old English Furniture shop.

In recent years much has been done to make sure the town's shop fronts are in keeping with the surrounding architecture. It was surely a case of the biggest and boldest possible in the 1920s. Then, Boots Cash Chemists was on the south side of the High Street. Further down you could not fail to miss the RESTAURANT sign at Brett's. The company was formerly known as Brett, Reynard & Co.

Richard Shillingford traded in Guildford for 67 years. Originally from Oxford, he first opened a grocer's shop (pictured here in about 1870) in the High Street in 1858. He also had an ironmonger's shop which he eventually sold in 1905, a china and earthenware business and at one time even acquired a butcher's shop. Shillingford was a strict Baptist and was one of the founder members of the small Baptist Church in The Bars, near Sandfield Terrace. He died, aged 87, in 1926.

At the turn of the century, Guildford had a number of chemists trading in the town. These included Henry Jeffries, Long & Co, F.Wheeler and, seen here, Waller Martin. Glass medicine bottles from this firm, dating from 1900-10, are embossed with the additional words 'T.L. Inman, MPS and Propr', the person who by that time owned the firm.

Near the corner of the High Street and Quarry Street were premises occupied by John Savage who traded as a hairdresser and as an antique furniture dealer. Next door is Adsetts, which made guns, rifles and revolvers.

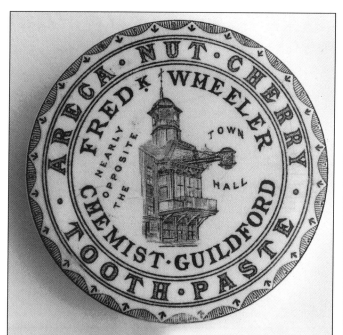

Many household commodities were packed and sold in shallow ceramic pots with lids printed with advertising. The mixture in Frederick Wheeler's Areca Nut Cherry Toothpaste would have contained a worming agent – although few Victorians would have realised it when cleaning their teeth. Note the delightful wording: 'Nearly opposite the Town Hall'. Mr Wheeler was in business from 1874 to 1904 and also had a mineral water works in Onslow Street. John William Savage had a hairdresser's shop at 103 High Street at about the turn of the century and must have sold plenty of pots of his Peruvian balm, as many examples have been dug from old refuse tips. Now a sought-after collectable, whether the hair restorer worked or not we will never know.

December 1905 and an amazing display of game hangs from the premises of Colebrook, fishmonger and poulterer, in the High Street.

A few doors up from the Guildhall was Stent & Clarke, printers and bookbinders. Signwriting just under the eaves in this 1922 picture states: ESTABD. 1765. IN THE REIGN OF GEORGE III. The firm was still in business well into the 1950s.

Moving on up the High Street, still on the Guildhall side, was the double-fronted entrance of Simpsons Bros. In a 1904 guidebook to the town, the firm advertised as a family linen warehouse. It also sold carpets, linoleums, floorcloths and Japanese and Indian rugs.

Dennis Bros

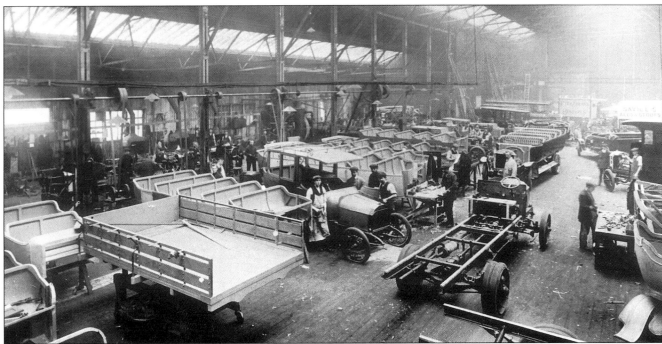

Guildford has been linked with motor vehicle engineering since the end of the nineteenth century. Thousands of lorries, buses, fire engines and municipal vehicles have been made in Guildford by Dennis for use at home and abroad. This picture shows a number of open charabancs and lorries being assembled at the Woodbridge Hill works in about 1920.

John Dennis came to Guildford from Bideford in Devon in 1894 to work for an ironmonger. In his spare time he made and sold bicycles and a year later set up his own business – the Universal Athletic Stores in the High Street. The 24-year-old engineer was joined by his younger brother, Raymond, and their bicycle manufacturing business soon turned to motorised vehicles. Being fined 20 shillings for riding his motor-tricycle up the High Street at 16mph worked in John Dennis's favour, as the publicity that followed certainly helped sales. Dennis Brothers Ltd was formed in 1901 and the firm moved from premises in the old North Street barracks to England's first purpose-built motor car factory on the corner of Onslow Street and Bridge Street. This picture, taken at Guildford railway station, shows one of the many Dennis cars made between 1900 and 1913, after which the firm concentrated on lorries, fire engines and buses.

Some of the workforce pictured with a Dennis lorry at the Onslow Street works just after World War One. The introduction in 1903 of Dennis's worm-drive rear axle set the firm apart from its rivals which were still using the less efficient and noisier chain drive method. In 1905, the firm expanded again, this time by purchasing the Torrey Alexander Mission Hall in Brixton, dismantling it and reassembling it on land at Woodbridge Hill. By 1909, some 400 people were employed at the two sites, and during the next three years the Woodbridge plant was expanded considerably.

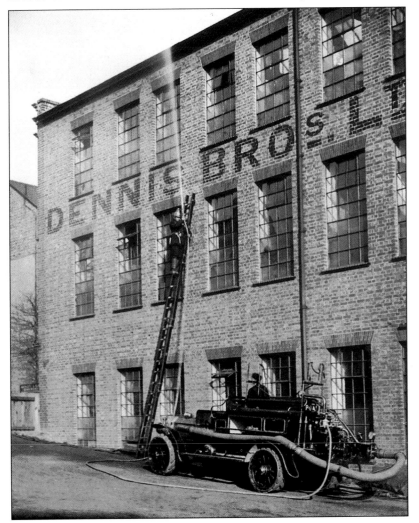

Another view of the Onslow Street site, now known as the Rodboro Buildings, with what looks like a test being carried out with a fire engine hose. During World War One, Dennis employed 1,400 men and women who built more than 7,000 three-ton lorries for the Government at an average of 20 a week. The firm also made pumps to supply drinking water on the Somme battlefield. And to combat the housing shortage in Guildford, following the company's growth, Dennis built 28 houses for its employees in Woking Road.

When finished, each Dennis vehicle was paraded for its official photograph. A number of locations in the borough were used. Here a fire engine, bound for Australia, is seen at the top of Woodbridge Hill at about the point where the A322 Worplesdon Road and A323 Aldershot Road meet today. The keep of Stoughton Barracks can be seen rising out of the mist.

This view shows part of the Woodbridge Hill site being built. As production here grew, the Onslow Street works became a repair shop. The 1920s were generally a difficult time for motor vehicle manufacturers. However, new models were developed and new markets opened up. While John Dennis stayed at home putting his creative engineering skills to work, brother Raymond embarked on a 60,000-mile world tour to drum up sales.

Gone now, but for many years a familiar sight was the frontage to the Dennis works at Woodbridge Hill. To the far left of the building was the works fire station. Offices formed the main part of the building, while to the right was the power house. The railway line to Waterloo is seen in the middle of the picture, while in the foreground the only buildings before Grays of Guildford and Plastic Coatings were built, was a public lavatory and the entrance to an air-raid shelter.

Inside the factory sometime during the 1920s and a line of lorries are being assembled. Note the huge piles of tyres stored at the far end of the workshop.

This photograph shows the extent of the Dennis factory. However, within this 'sea' of industrial buildings there was still greenery – note the trees forming a natural barrier between the workshop buildings. The A3 can be seen in the background.

Many types of commercial vehicles were made. Here, factory workers queue to see if the vehicle designed as a mobile dispenser of Lyons' coffee comes up to scratch. A loud speaker has been placed on the cab roof. Was this used to attract custom in the same way as the tune played by ice-cream vans?

Spot the locations used by the Dennis photographer: A street cleaning vehicle makes a good job of spraying its jets of water along Recreation Road.

Crowds come out to see a Dennis tarring machine make its way up New Cross Road in Stoughton. Although thick, black smoke blocks out any significant landmarks, the houses on the right confirm the location. The homes which form Martin Road and Franks Road were later built on the land to the left.

After Raymond and John Dennis died within three months of each other in 1938, aged 59 and 67, respectively, changes followed, and, with the outbreak of World War Two, the firm went into full-time production, 24 hours a day, making a range of products for the war effort, which included Churchill tanks, trailer pumps for fire-fighting, armoured personnel carriers and bomb assemblies. In this picture, a tank is being made ready for its rail journey out of the Dennis sidings. Note the camouflage paint applied to the roofs of the buildings which, perhaps, prevented them from being hit by the Luftwaffe.

Some 3,000 people were employed at the factory during the war. The majority were local, but buses brought in workers from as far afield as London. Women worked alongside men in departments such as the machine shop, as seen here. Romances were struck up and many marriages followed.

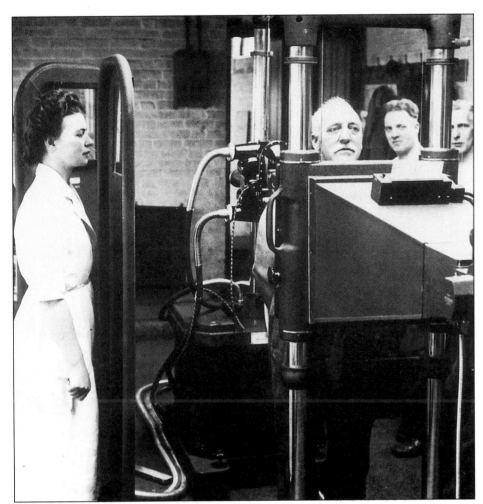

Keeping the employees healthy was important to ensure production remained high. The man having a chest X-ray has been identified as Mr Clarke, who not only had a managerial position in the factory but dressed up as Santa Claus for the employees' children's parties during the 1930s!

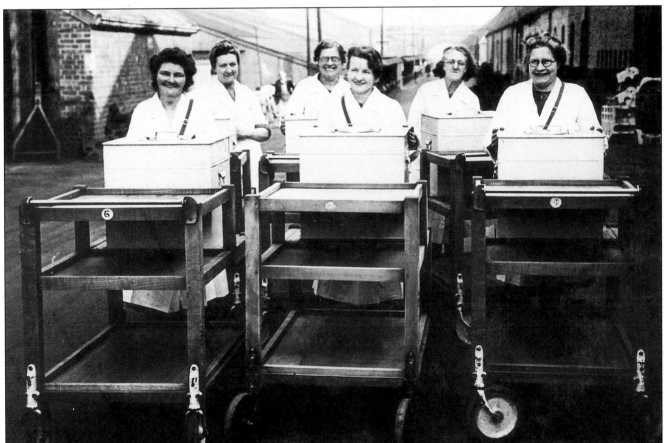

Tea up, lads! The smiling faces of these women as they served refreshments must have helped a long shift on the workshop pass more quickly.

Dennis's canteen and the tables have been laid out for what looks like a party. Although it served as a place of recreation where people could sit and talk, note the sign high up on the wall. It says: GAMBLING STRICTLY PROHIBITED.

The end of another shift: This 1940s view looks along the main entrance with workers walking towards Midleton Road. The blacksmith's and the hardening shop were in the building on the lower right. In front of the sawmill and body shop (also on the right) can be seen a very long bicycle shed. By the end of the 1980s the firm had transferred to Slyfield where it is still making high-quality specialist vehicles. The Woodbridge Hill site has been redeveloped into a modern business park.

Bringing You The News

The first edition of the *Surrey Advertiser and Commercial and Agricultural Register* appeared on 2 April 1864. Circulated gratuitously, it was the brainchild of a businessman in the town, Joseph Whittaker Barfoot.

Joseph Whittaker Barfoot, the founder of the *Surrey Advertiser*, was a man of many trades. He ran his Paperhanging and Decorative Warehouse from 10 High Street, Guildford. He was listed as an accountant, estate agent and valuer, and the secretary of the West Surrey Permanent Mutual Benefit Building Society. The new venture was no more than an eight-page advertising sheet, but by July of that year local news and articles were being included.

In November 1867, Barfoot sold the newspaper to Alexander Forsythe Asher and Angus Fraser Walbrook. Moving briefly to, first, Farnham Road and then Sydenham Road, the ever-growing company settled in Market Street, where its offices and printing works were to remain for 65 years. Following Mr Asher's death on Boxing Day 1916, members of his family continued to run the business and, in the spring of 1937, with Jack Harrison, a grandson, in control, moved to its present purpose-built premises in Martyr Road. Here, we see the building of reinforced concrete faced with cream faience tiles suitably decorated for the coronation of Queen Elizabeth II in 1953.

The *Surrey Advertiser* had as its rival the *Surrey Times*, which was based at the Woodbridge Press in Onslow Street. Pictured in 1922 are members of the two newspapers who took part in a cricket match. A note written on the back of the photograph records that the match was won by the *Advertiser*.

A glimpse of Martyr Road before the *Surrey Advertiser* took up residence. A.Hart & Sons sold its nursery business to W. & J.Spooner in 1923. The cottage and greenhouses were demolished in 1928. The *Surrey Advertiser* building was started in 1936 and took nine months to complete. The architect was Leslie Hiscock, of Guildford, and the general contractors were Hall, Beddall & Co, of London. There were no fewer than 22 sub-contractors employed in addition to those supplying and erecting the machinery.

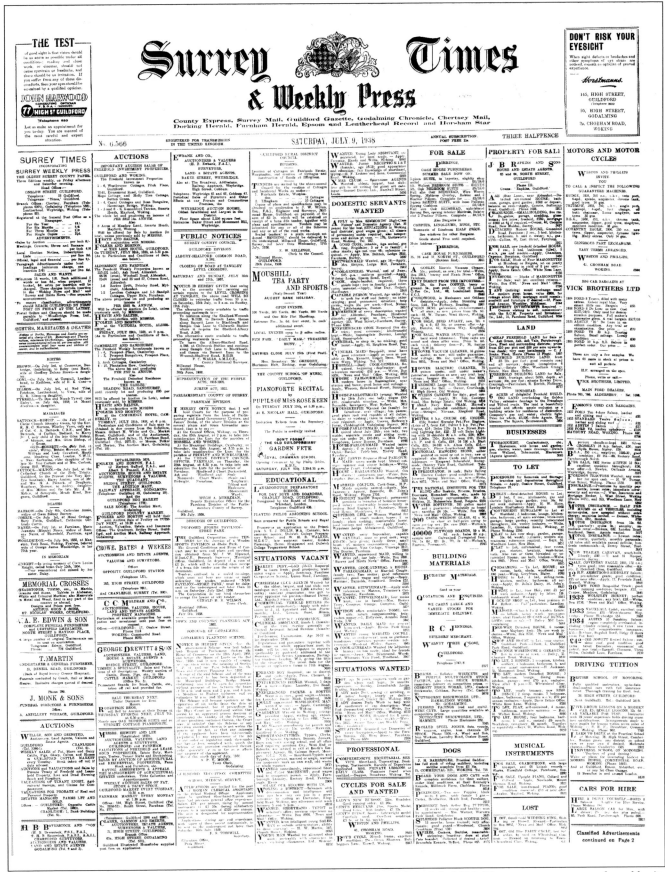

A newspaper from the past: The *Surrey Times & Weekly Press* looked like this in July 1938. The company was purchased by its rival in 1964, and the first part of the title reappeared in 1981 when the *Advertiser* launched its midweek free series.

How the newsroom looked in 1964. From the left we see the chief reporter, Tony Welby, and reporters Peter Pallot, Penny Owen and Vic Peters. The editorial department was situated on the first floor of the Martyr Road building. Expansion of the company in the 1970s saw the journalists move out and, since 1977, they have been based in Pannells Court, off Chertsey Street. Typewriters remained in use in the newsroom until 1991 when they were replaced by computers.

In the hot metal days of printing, before the advent of computer technology, the reporters' typewritten copy, after being checked by the sub-editors, would pass to the typesetters. This late 1960s photo *(left)* shows a Linotype machine in the foreground. A melting lead ingot can be seen attached to a chain on the left, while to the left of the operator, Eric Antao, freshly made lines of type can be seen.

The many pieces of metal type, pictures and advertisements have been 'composed' into a page. Platemaker Ralph Brewser 'planes the type' to ensure it is level and flat before a final stereo plate is made and attached to the press.

The press in Martyr Road was in daily use, printing other titles in the Surrey Advertiser group as well as contract jobs, such as the *Jewish Chronicle*. Therefore newsprint was delivered each morning. Some considerable skill was needed by the lorry drivers, in manoeuvring their vehicles as close to the building as possible, and by the machine room staff, whose job it was to unload the heavy rolls, which weighed as much as one ton, before lowering them to a storeroom beneath the press hall.

Advertisements taken at random from the pages of the *Surrey Advertiser* in days gone by.

The *Surrey Advertiser's* Goss Headliner press soon after it was installed in 1961. This machine printed the newspapers until August 1992 when, sadly, a decision was taken to discontinue printing in Guildford after 128 years.

A 1970s glimpse of the press hall. By now computers and photo-typesetters had replaced the hot metal machines. Lines of type and advertisements were output on bromide paper, waxed and then pasted on to the pages. A film negative was made in order to produce a flexible metal plate which was attached to the press on drums, one of which was under the metal cover shown here.

Guildford EVENING ADVERTISER

THURSDAY, JANUARY 25, 1968

A model boat, a reminder of the past, takes shape today in the hands of a future generation of sailors—boys of St. Thomas of Canterbury Primary School, Merrow. Meanwhile, at North Korea, the world's largest warship, the U.S. nuclear-powered aircraft carrier, Enterprise, (right) awaits developments in the crisis surrounding her sister ship, the U.S.S. Pueblo.

Big tax frauds exposed

SNAP tests of claims for personal reliefs from tax for dependants show that about half the sample cases were fraudulent, the Comptroller and Auditor General, Sir Bruce Fraser, says today.

The principal method of evading tax, according to the report, is to claim for non-existent dependants who are overseas.

In practice, he says, inspectors of taxes often accept, without further investigation, Declarations of Entitlement in respect of these reliefs, but in April, 1966 the Inland Revenue decided to institute a pilot scheme to test the validity of claims and to determine whether such a scheme could be applied generally.

About 1,000 claimants, selected from 20 tax districts, were asked for Certificates of Registration of Births and Marriages, which were then investigated for their authenticity.

By January, 1967, says Sir Bruce, it was clear that the proportion of fraudulent claims for non-resident dependants was high and by October, 1967, a further review suggested that around 35 per cent of the claims in the sample were fraudulent.

This indicated an overall loss of tax due to fraudulent claims of between £5 million and £7 million a year and a cumulative loss to date of about four times that amount.

'CONFESSIONS'

As the result of an announcement in June that the Inland Revenue would not prosecute anyone who admitted false claims to personal allowances by September 30th 1967, 1,400 'confessions' were made.

Sir Bruce says the Inland Revenue does not consider it practicable to extend the so-called inquiries being made to the pilot scheme to the whole field of suspect personal allowance claims.

Sir Bruce also said it had been found that in several cases employers entitled to Selective Employment Tax premiums and refunds had claimed and been paid the money after certifying that tax had been paid, whereas, in fact, some or all of the tax had not been paid.

The Ministry of Labour informed him that a fully safeguarded system was not possible without a considerable increase in staff at the ministry and at the Ministry of Social Security.

A system of checking on National Insurance card payments is being introduced as one method of checking on the entitlement of the employer to a repayment of tax and a premium.

NOW HIGHER TELEPHONE CHARGES?

INCREASES in telephone charges, forecast by the Postmaster-General, Mr. Edward Short, appear to have been discussed at today's meeting of the Cabinet.

Guildford EVENING ADVERTISER is an experimental newspaper, published for five days only. Its contents are a token of those which would be in a larger, regular "Evening Advertiser." See page 7.

It is possible also that plans for increasing the television licence fee, for which the B.B.C. has been asking, were also on the agenda.

Mr. Short, who is not a member of the Cabinet, was one of the three additional ministers called in to today's meeting.

He was a constant attender also at the series of Cabinet meetings which produced the Government's programme of economic cuts from which the Post Office was specifically excluded.

While economies in public spending may not affect the Post Office which in any event is to become a public corporation, one way of avoiding any necessity to subsidise the department would be to introduce profit-making increases.

With Mr Short at today's meeting were the Chief Secretary to the Treasury, Mr. John Diamond, who is responsible for controlling public expenditure, and the Attorney General, Sir Elwyn Jones.

The Prime Minister, freshly back from Moscow, presided and all other Cabinet Ministers were present.

IT MAY COST MORE AT LIDO

SUBJECT to approval of Guildford Town Council next Tuesday, entrance charges to the Lido open-air swimming pool are to be doubled next season.

In a review of the charges at both the Lido and the Castle Street Baths, the public ground committee is recommending new charges from the start of the summer season of 2s. weekdays and 1s. Sundays and Bank Holidays for adults. The current charges are 1s. and 1s. 6d. respectively.

Children under 15 years will also have to find double the money and pay next season 1s. on weekdays and 1s. 6d. on Sundays and Bank Holidays.

Season tickets, the committee recommends, should be increased from 10s. to 45s. for adults and from £1 to 25s. for children. The cost of hiring the pool for special events should be 50s. instead of the present 25s., and 2d. should be added to the current charge of 4d. for deckchairs.

The committee is recommending no change for Castle Street Baths.

G.L.C. spending up by £9m.

The first four Greater London Council committees to produce their 1968-69 estimates anticipate a total increase of £9,589,450 in capital and revenue spending compared with the present year.

All four sets of estimates, to be considered by the council on Tuesday, were prepared before the Government's recently announced economic measures.

The £4,209,450 jump in the revenue account estimates would have to be found from rates. But a G.L.C. spokesman pointed out today that Mr. Desmond Plummer, the council's leader, had said that they hoped no increase in the rates would be necessary.

Rent-free tenant left £27 damage

FOR 11 months, Mrs. Gilberte Appleby lived in a flat above a shop in Quarry Street, Guildford, where she worked. And when she resigned last April, she left £27 worth of damage to furniture, and took £12 17s. 6d. holiday pay which she said was due to her.

At Guildford County Court today, Judge Lionel Jellinek awarded judgment of £12 2s. against Mrs. Appleby, in favour of her former employers, Earrington Kennels, Alton.

Mr. George Atkinson representing the company, said Mrs. Appleby, who now lives in Brighton occupied the flat rent free. She took £9 12s. 6d. more holiday pay than was due to her, and damaged furniture which was in perfectly good condition when she took the flat.

Mr. Atkinson said there was also a cooker which she had taken out when she moved in and which she had not reinstated. To reinstate it had cost him £1 6s. 6d.

Fined £5

Edward Elwick, of 9 Gravel Pit Cottages, Gomshall, was fined £5 by Godalming magistrates today (Thursday) for parking without lights.

40 Friary workers to lose jobs

DUE to the proposed closure of the bottling department at the Friars Meux Brewery, Guildford, about 40 employees will become redundant.

Of the 40 redundancies, which will come into effect some time after Easter, 32 will be female employees. A spokesman for Ind Coope Breweries, who took over Friary Meux a few years ago, said that many of the workers in the bottling plant would be absorbed in other departments of the Guildford brewery.

The closure of the bottling plant was said the spokesman, a matter of rationalisation and economics. Ind Coope had other breweries in the area which could cope with bottling. He said also that the trend in brewing is towards draught beer and there has been a slackening off in trade in bottled beer.

Michael Barnett, of 50 Spring Grove, Farncombe, was fined £1 by Godalming magistrates today (Thursday) for parking without obligatory lights.

Wet or fine?

Forecast for the period 6 a.m. to midnight tomorrow.

London area, south - east England: rather cloudy with some rain in places at first. Some bright intervals later.

Wind west to north - west, moderate.

Temperature rather above normal. Maximum 8C (46F.)

LOTTERY WINS MAY BEAT THE POOLS

ANNOUNCING the National Lottery Bill, published today, its sponsor, Mr. James Tinn (Labour, Cleveland), said at a London news conference that he envisaged prizes higher than the largest pools wins and many smaller prizes of about £500 or £750.

"It is possible that about £2 million a week may be spent by the punter. There is bound to be a certain switch from the pools," he said.

"The odds will be very fair and the punter who loses will have at least the consolation that most of his loss will have gone for medical purposes."

The Bill, which comes up for its second reading on February 2nd authorises the creation of a national lottery board to organise and operate the scheme and to make grants to charitable organisations, medical research, and for other social and welfare purposes.

Mr. Tinn said the Bill did not attempt to give in detail the method of operation, size of prizes, frequency of draws or similar matters.

The week the weekly became an evening: The *Guildford Evening Advertiser* appeared for five days in January 1968 to warn predatory newspaper publishers they would have a fight on their hands if they attempted to move into the heart of Surrey.

Once the pages had been printed, each newspaper was automatically folded and trimmed before emerging from the press. Bundles of newspapers then travelled by conveyor belt to another part of the press hall where they were bound and labelled for their destinations at newsagents and wholesalers. Seen here are printers George Comfort (left) and Ted Saunders.

Newspapers being tied and bundled in the 1960s by Millie Millward, who worked for the *Surrey Advertiser* for many years. In 1979, the company was sold to the *Guardian* and *Manchester Evening News*, now known as the Guardian Media Group. Ray Tindle, who had joined the firm in 1962 as managing director, succeeded Dr John Murray as chairman. Knighted in 1994, Sir Ray retired in 1997.

And where would any newspaper be without its paper boys and girls delivering it directly to the readers' doorsteps? A 1970s line up of some of those who delivered the *Surrey Daily Advertiser*, launched in October 1974 to fight off fierce competition in the industry, and which continued until April 1980. Since then it has been the county's biggest weekly newspaper, and is now in three broadsheet sections with a tabloid leisure and TV guide, plus regular supplements and inserts. The latest techniques in computer publishing technology are used by both editorial and advertising staff, and finished pages are sent by telecommunication lines to the full colour press at Reading. Not only can it be read in traditional form, excerpts are now available to internet users all over the world on the *Advertiser's* web site.

Lost Guildford

The car is turning left from Farnham Road into Bridge Street, or maybe the railway station, a manoeuvre that, since road widening, can now only be made with the aid of traffic lights. The Napoleon Hotel started life as the Emperor Napoleon III in about 1855 and its nameplate displays the familiar red and black of the Guildford brewery Friary Meux. Soon after the pub became vacant and derelict the whole block was demolished in the 1980s to make way for offices and a YMCA. The double decker Aldershot & District Traction Co bus is heading down Farnham Road for the bus station beside the river. In front of the bus is the building, long since gone, which had housed the technical school before Guildford Technical College was built in Stoke Road.

Pulled down in 1963, the Railway Hotel was situated close to the entrance to the railway station, where Park Street, Bridge Street, Farnham Road and Walnut Tree Close meet. There is a pedestrian subway at the site today.

The top of Bridge Street before redevelopment in the early 1960s. The derelict buildings were demolished to make way for Bridge House which became the Post Office's Guildford telephone area headquarters until it was moved to purpose-built offices in Aldershot in 1984. Coombs's garage was owned by John Coombs, well-known in motor racing after World War Two, whose family had started as wheelwrights in the late 1880s. Coombs also had premises on Portsmouth Road at St Catherine's and on the bypass at Stag Hill, south of the cathedral. After the Post Office moved out, Bridge House, which had been designed by the prominent Guildford architect John Brownrigg, whose other work included the Yvonne Arnaud Theatre, remained empty for three years until a planning wrangle between the borough council and the site owners, Norwich Union, was resolved. Then the demolition crew got to work, and in time a new £10 million Bridge House, again designed by the firm of Scott, Brownrigg & Turner, rose from the ashes. This is now occupied by the Government Office for the South East. It is difficult to believe that this quiet scene is now part of the one-way gyratory system that has so bedevilled Guildford in the last 15 years. The vandalised buildings were in Railway Esplanade which once ran into the then cul-de-sac of Walnut Tree Close.

Looking up The Mount in the 1950s. The building on the right is still there, now occupied by a firm of estate agents while, diagonally opposite, the offices at 2 High Street, on the corner of Portsmouth Road and Bury Fields, was occupied by estate agents Gascoigne-Pees. The Weyside Temperance Hotel began life as the Welcome Coffee Tavern just before the turn of the century and was demolished shortly after this photograph was taken to make way for two blocks of flats whose presence continues to be a blot on the landscape. In addition to the post-war cars in the photograph, mainly varieties of Morris and Ford, the road signs and the overhead street light make this a particularly poignant image of bygone Guildford.

Friary Street about 1960, looking towards High Street, when it was the A281 and an important thoroughfare for traffic before the building of Millbrook. The Bear pub on the left was one of Guildford's oldest hostelries and was sold by Courage in 1964 to pave the way for redevelopment into the pedestrians only shopping street it is today. On the right can be seen the Esso sign above the Friary garage of Court & Smith, which is now based just off the A3 at Burnt Common, Send.

Who remembers these Friary Street shops? From the right, E.M.Downes, fruiterer; Peter B.Harris, tobacconist; L.Barton & Son, fishmonger and poulterer; The Wool Shop; and The Friary Cafe. The lorry belonging to The Furniture Mart may have been delivering goods to Ye Olde Curiosity Shoppe, owned by Mr V.G.Trower, at 5 Friary Street.

To work this one out, stand with your back to the North Street entrance to the Friary Centre and look across to what is now Phoenix Court. Most of the buildings were demolished during the redevelopment of Friary Street, which is off to the right, in the late 1960s, although the London plane tree survived until December 1980.

Guildford's very own hole in the wall – the old militia barracks at the bottom of North Street and Friary Street was, by the time this photograph was taken in about 1950, let out to various businesses. There are vivid memories of it always being wet under the arch, and anyone old enough will certainly recall the shop Buyers – in which every nook and cranny was filled with all manner of second-hand goods.

A picture postcard view of The Mortuary, Guildford. Two clues to its location are the steps, bottom right, which would appear to be Rosemary Alley between Quarry Street and Millbrook, and, top left, the tower and clock face of St Mary's Church. This would place the corporation-owned mortuary on the site of the present Bellairs studio opposite the entrance to the Yvonne Arnaud Theatre.

A town centre scene that will be unrecognisable to all but the older residents with good memories. It was taken in 1962 when traffic could turn left or right into the High Street from Millbrook. Opposite, vehicles emerging from Friary Street could also turn left or right or, if the destination was Shalford or beyond, go straight over the crossroads and continue along the A281.

The White Lion Walk shopping arcade is the only reminder of the once great Lion Hotel. Dating back to at least 1593, the coaching inn dominated this part of the High Street. The façade seen in this 1900s view came about in stages of rebuilding throughout the nineteenth century. Its 1925 brochure boasted 60 bedrooms but in 1957 it was pulled down and replaced by a Woolworths store.

Tunsgate in the late 1950s. This rarely glimpsed view shows the car park on the left that preceded the commercial buildings and, much later, Tunsgate Square. The tall building on the left is Harveys department store in the High Street, now Army & Navy.

It can be clearly seen just how narrow the High Street was where the Ram Inn stood. Even at this time, when motor transport was in its infancy, it was considered a hindrance to traffic and was therefore demolished in 1913.

The demolition of Ram Corner in this April 1913 view taken from where Chertsey Street joins North Street.

Allen House stood opposite the Royal Grammar School in the upper High Street. It was built in about 1660 by Thomas Cranfield and had a large elegant garden. Seen here in about 1920, it was demolished to make way for an expanding grammar school in 1964.

A parade of shops in the upper High Street in the 1920s. On the right can be seen Rita, ladies' outfitters. The modern building on this site today is home to the Argos store.

From these ashes came the Yvonne Arnaud Theatre. Shortly after 5 o'clock in the morning of 24 April 1963, North Street Theatre erupted like a volcano. A loud explosion woke people living in the town centre, and soon sheets of flame and palls of smoke were issuing from the Co-operative Society-owned building in Leapale Road, where there had been a repertory theatre since 1946. Guildford's first theatre, in Market Street, had been demolished in 1889, and the subsequent Theatre Royal had operated from 1912 to its closure in 1933. The building pictured had been the Borough Halls and assize court until its conversion in 1946. Work on the Yvonne Arnaud Theatre, on its riverside site, was already under way when the fire broke out.

A view through the window of one of the artisans' villas in North Place built between the 1830s and 1840s. These houses were pulled down in 1972, but not quite everything ended up in the builder's skip. For as long as he can remember, Guildford man Charles Brooking has had a passion for collecting old architectural artefacts, such as door knockers, sash windows, staircases and lumps of ironmongery. Luckily he was in the right place at the right time to salvage bits of Guildford's past from buildings such as the Friary Brewery, the railway station, houses in Woodbridge Road, Falcon Road and Bedford Road as they were reduced to rubble. The majority of his collection, now numbering more than 50,000 items, is housed at the University of Greenwich in Dartford, Kent. It is open to the public by appointment.

The Live and Let Live pub is the only easily recognisable feature in this part of North Place. It started life as a beerhouse in the 1860s. Next door, the property with the bay window was the draper's shop of Miss E.Burdett. The cottages in the foreground were knocked down to make way for Guildford Youth Centre, and those in the background, between the pub and Beverley Hall, were cleared for old people's accommodation.

At one time there were many substantial properties along Woodbridge Road, but by the 1960s some had become run down. This is Wellington Place seen standing in front of the then new police station.

The Horse and Groom pub can just be seen through the end of this passage way leading into North Street. The structure forming the overhead walkway dated from the end of the seventeenth century and was demolished in 1974.

Yet another town centre car park stands where these 1854-built police houses stood on the east side of Leapale Road. This view is from the mid-1970s. Note the once ubiquitous Hillman Avenger car parked in the street.

Looking towards Eagle Road in the 1970s after the demolition men had been at work. A block of nineteenth century cottages had been cleared for new homes.

These Victorian villas in Stoke Road, seen here in the mid-1970s, were soon to succumb to the demolition contractor's ball and chain. However, housing for the elderly has been built in their place in a style sympathetic to neighbouring buildings.

Rookwood House, shown in both views here, off the Portsmouth Road, was built in about 1835. Enlarged in 1863, it was the rectory of St Nicolas Church. It became a private house in 1970 but only survived another three years before it was pulled down.

Dating from the 1840s, this villa once stood at the corner of Stoke Road and York Road. It was another victim of the mid-1970s demolition programme in the town.

Guildford and the Friary Brewery were synonymous for about 100 years. This building in Commercial Road was one of the town's most prominent landmarks until its demolition at the end of 1973. Guildford was a town of many breweries, but by World War Two only the Friary remained. For decades it was known as Friary Holroyd and Healy, but in 1965 it merged with Meux to become Friary Meux and signalled the beginning of the end for smaller breweries. Allied Breweries, which had been formed in 1961, took over Friary Meux through its Ind Coope title in 1963, and its Romford brewery assumed greater importance. Guildford's last brew took place on 23 December 1968, and when the Commercial Road premises were sold to MEPC it was the start of the end of an era. The tower was demolished, at the second attempt, on Sunday, 17 February 1974.

An early 1970s view looking down Bridge Street towards Onslow Street showing the entrance to the wholesale order department building of the Friary Brewery which was built in 1895. It was in that year that the brewery, trading as Friary Holroyd & Healy, was formed into a limited company.

Soon to be pulled down, this is a view from Commercial Road of the Friary's bottling factory built in about 1926.

The bitter end: The Friary Brewery tower comes crashing to the ground in 1974.

A secret garden! Within the brewery complex was this garden tended by the caretaker and his wife, Mr and Mrs Orr. The directors' offices looked out on to it.

Commercial Street in 1974 with the 1897-built part of the Friary Brewery. Note the firing slits in the wartime gun emplacements.

This interesting view of Onslow Street shows the rather ornate building of Shelvey's Mineral Water Works while Guildford Gas Works can just be seen on the right. The buildings on the left were demolished in the 1970s to make way for the Friary Centre.

The making of the Friary Centre in the early 1970s. These shops were in Onslow Street, facing Bedford Road. The only business still open was Relics Antiques, owned by Arthur Atkinson. Next-door neighbours Heathorns Turf Accountants had been boarded up, but older residents will recall the days when you could have a shave for one shilling and a hair cut and brush, by machinery, for threepence.

The terraced cottages known as Ivy Place in Chertsey Street are still here but the little shop on the corner of Martyr Road has long gone. During World War Two it was a cobbler's shop, then it became a barber's shop before ending its life as an antiques emporium.

Sydenham Road multi-storey car park now stands on the site once occupied by this tile-hung building. Seen here as Stent & Co's printers and bookbinders, it was, from at least the end of the sixteenth century until about 1920, a pub going under the various names of the Bell and Trumpet, the Trumpet, and finally the Queen's Head.

An Edwardian view of a group of buildings which once stood at the bottom of Quarry Street. The hanging sign is outside the Good Intent Lodging House.

Many residents still call the roundabout at the junction of London Road and the A25 the AA roundabout, even though Fanum House has disappeared. The Automobile Association's regional offices were built in 1934, to replace those at Ram Corner in the town centre, and during the war housed the organisation's London-based records in a specially reinforced air-raid shelter at the rear of the building. The clock tower, made by Braby, a leading zinc manufacturer in London, has been retained on the present building.

Guildford Power Station in Woodbridge Road was built in 1928 and closed in 1968. It was pulled down in January 1969.

The south-east view of Stoke Park House taken during the early 1920s when it was in use as a school. Built at the end of the eighteenth century by William Aldersey, it had a succession of owners, including the 4th Earl of Onslow. It remained a school until World War Two, after which it became part of Guildford Technical College. There was much protest when it was demolished in 1977.

A rare view of the long demolished Woodbridge House, which stood in Woodbridge Road, a short distance from its junction with Stocton Road. One wonders whether the photographer deliberately composed the picture with the little girl sitting in the long grass in the foreground.

Almost a quarter of a century ago, and what a difference. This was the junction of Midleton Road and Woodbridge Hill with the A3 in February 1976. The houses were demolished when the trunk road was elevated. The stretch of the former A3, where the vehicles are waiting for the traffic lights to change, is now known as Midleton Road up to the Dennis roundabout.

A February 1976 view of Deerbarn Road, Woodbridge Hill, looking down towards Hestair Dennis with the cathedral in the background. Today, this part of Guildford has changed almost beyond recognition. The houses on the right and those further down the road on the left were demolished when the new by-pass, roundabout and link roads were built in the 1980s. The poplar trees went along with all the Dennis buildings shortly afterwards to make way for a business park.

The Building of Today's Town

Warwick's Bench at about the time of World War One, with the road laid out prior to it being developed with its large detached homes. It has become a favourite alternative route for motorists attempting to beat the traffic jams in the town centre.

The draper's shop of John Reeks & Co was destroyed by fire on 5 November 1915. The site remained derelict until, shortly before the end of World War One, when it was cleared by Canadian soldiers from Witley camp who transformed it into a mock-up of a front-line trench system, known as 'Flanders by Moonlight'. The big event was Feed the Guns Week from 21-26 October 1918, and the promoters set themselves the target of raising £250,000 from the sale of War Bonds and War Savings Certificates. By the end of the first day, £90,000 had been subscribed, and by the Friday night the total was £225,000. Banks and other big concerns were mainly responsible for this amount. The two local companies, Dennis Bros and the Friary Brewery, gave £20,000 and £10,000 respectively, while Friary employees contributed £2,365, and the boys of the Royal Grammar School collected £1,360. The site was cleared in 1919 in preparation for the Picture Playhouse.

The Caxton Housing Scheme was an early attempt to provide affordable homes for the workers. Billing & Sons, once a major printing company in Guildford, having secured land in Weston Road, off Woodbridge Hill, in 1906, formed the Caxton Gardens Cottage Club. It was aware that rents for small houses in the town had reached, on average, 'a distinctly higher level than in many other towns of similar character'. The aim was to provide employees with modern cottages at a reasonable rent and on terms which would enable them to buy their properties. Building was completed in 1907 and by 1924 all 24 tenants had bought their homes and the scheme was terminated. Seen on the left of the bottom picture are houses in Weston Road. The section of the A3 where it passes over the Wooden Bridge (Dennis) roundabout is behind these properties today.

The Picture Playhouse was an arcade with shops, a theatre, a club and Winter Gardens designed by Frederick Hodgson and built between 1919-21 at a cost of £60,000. The façade was mock-Tudor and blended well with the older buildings in the High Street. The link between the two has been removed and the arcade was much renovated in the 1980s to create Tunsgate Square shopping centre, sold this year for £16.6 million.

Excavations are taking place for the Picture Playhouse. The playhouse opened in 1922 and the manager was Henry Mills. In September 1929 County Cinemas took on the lease and later Odeon Theatres Ltd secured the controlling interest. When Mr Mills retired, aged 84, in April 1943, he was succeeded by Basil Putt but continued as the company secretary. Mr Putt was one of the youngest managers on the Odeon circuit and had previously been at the Plaza in Guildford. Subsequently, he became house manager at the Odeon in Leicester Square.

The Winter Gardens were entered from the arcade. Guildford Picture Playhouse and Winter Gardens Ltd, the company which owned the Playhouse cinema, accepted a 'very substantial offer' to sell the building to one of the lessees, M.Faiman Ltd, a women's fashion shop, towards the end of 1962. The cinema, however, continued until its final films, *The Bulldog Breed* and *The Square Peg*, starring Norman Wisdom, on 12 June 1965. The Playhouse was demolished the following year and replaced by a supermarket. Tunsgate Square was built in 1972 and greatly enhanced in the 1980s.

A glass roof let light stream into the first-floor café of the Picture Playhouse.

A glimpse of the Picture Playhouse arcade itself leading to the Winter Gardens. On the right can be seen the premises of William Harvey, the outfitters, which had started life in 1919 in temporary accommodation in the Old Corn Exchange (Tunsgate Arch). Mr Harvey was the Mayor of Guildford from 1931-33 and on his death a private limited company was formed. The firm moved across the High Street in 1948 and three years later Harveys became a public company. It was bought by Army & Navy Stores in 1953, and underwent several extensions, the most notable of which was the addition in 1956 of a sixth floor rooftop water garden designed by the celebrated architect Geoffrey Jellicoe.

A view of the Picture Playhouse theatre/cinema from the balcony.

Shortly after World War One a national building programme was started to provide council-owned homes. Shepherds Hill in Stoughton was one of the earliest developments in the borough of Guildford. This view was taken in 1920 as the homes neared completion. Work has started on landscaping the paths and gardens. Note the young saplings which have just been planted. Some have now grown into mature trees. The estate was designed by Guildford architect Edward Lunn who succeeded Henry Peak. Mr Lunn was joined by Frederick Hodgson in a firm that continued the important work of shaping the town centre of which so much remains today. Mr Hodgson played a key role in the life of the town, including Guildford City Football Club, and was succeeded in business by his son, John, and more latterly by his grandson, Christopher.

Onslow Village in its infancy. The descriptive booklet issued by Onslow Village Ltd in June 1924 stated that the object of the Onslow Village Society was to develop the estate on garden city lines. The company was registered on 20 February 1920, as the country began to grapple with social problems in the immediate post-war period. One of the greatest needs was housing as men returned from the front. Guildford was no exception and the Earl of Onslow's generous offer of 646 acres at £57 per acre – approximately 25% of the market value – was quickly accepted. Lord Onslow, grandfather of the present earl, also invested £6,000 into the project. Herbert Powell, of Littleton, Guildford, chairman of the county council who also became chairman of the Onslow Village board of management, put in £4,000 and the borough council loaned £20,000 under the terms of the 1919 Housing Act. The foundation stones were laid for the first pair of cottages to be built, at Crossways, at a rain-soaked ceremony on Saturday, 1 May 1920. The Mayor of Guildford, Mr W.S. Tavener, said that 10 months earlier Guildford had been the first municipality to start a housing scheme, and now it was a pioneer in co-operating with an organisation called Co-partnership Tenants Ltd. It was originally planned to build 1,000 houses on a square-mile site, but over the years the plan for the village, as a self-contained community, was pared back to what it is today – a leafy suburb which made national headlines in 1984 when Onslow Village Ltd pre-empted the Conservative Government's Right to Buy legislation by selling up and offering its 231 shareholders the opportunity to buy their properties at knockdown prices.

Work in progress on the Friary Shopping Centre in 1979. This was a period when so many of the old, familiar commercial premises, long past their useful life, were ripped down to make way for the new trend of shopping arcades and malls. It was a time that was to alter once and for all the way we shopped and traded.

The hole that became the Friary Centre. Little has changed in the immediate neighbourhood of the building site, although Onslow Street bus station has made way for contract parking and the Electric Theatre. The prominent shape of the Rodboro Buildings, which started life as the first Dennis Brothers factory, is unmistakable. Bridge House, at the top right of the picture, was built about 1960 and was generally regarded as an eyesore. It was demolished in 1988 to make way for the present building of the same name which is occupied by the Government Office for the South East.

All the fun of the fair on the derelict Friary site before development of the shopping centre began in the mid-1970s.

Archaeologists working on the site of the erstwhile Dominican Friary as it began to be transformed into the modern day shopping centre in the 1970s. This photograph was taken in June 1974. The building at the top left was part of the Plaza, and is now a nightclub. In the centre background are terraced properties in Onslow Street waiting to be demolished. Beyond them are the Bedford Road flats and the police station. To the right are St Saviour's Church and the buildings in Woodbridge Road and Commercial Road.

A View From Above

There have been numerous changes to central Guildford since this aerial view was taken in the 1950s. Key landmarks are Holy Trinity Church in the foreground and the shops and offices forming a V at the junction of Epsom and London Roads at the top. The open space on the left was then Allen House and its grounds, now occupied by the Royal Grammar School. The Civic Hall had not been built nor had the multi-storey car park in Sydenham Road.

Debenhams' store dominates this view taken during the September 1968 floods. Clearly seen is the Yvonne Arnaud Theatre, the Castle Keep, the High Street, part of North Street and the massive car park in Sydenham Road.

Looking west across the town with the railway station in the centre of the picture, the houses of Onslow Village and Guildford Park stretching out to open fields, and the new university buildings beginning to cover Stag Hill.

The roof of the engine shed forming a crescent stands out on the left of this picture, although the last steam locomotive had departed more than a year before in July 1967. The town mill is dwarfed by Debenhams and the Yvonne Arnaud Theatre.

This superb aerial shot taken on Whit Monday in 1966 shows the preparatory work being undertaken for what was to become the University of Surrey campus beside the cathedral on Stag Hill. In the middle distance, Guildford Cricket Club 2nd XI is on its way to beating Ottershaw II on the Woodbridge Road sports ground while, across the railway line, Old Guildfordians CC is playing and defeating Guildford City Supporters on the Recreation Road ground. Further to the left can be seen the Guildford City Football Club ground in Josephs Road. Surrey County Show, which attracted a crowd of 70,000, is in full swing in Stoke Park at the top of the photograph.

A good 1960s aerial view of the Aldershot & District Traction Co bus garage and the Morris Depot in Woodbridge Road. Above the centrally placed bus garage can be seen Ingram, Perkins & Co's timber yard.

The power station in Woodbridge Road is at the centre of this view. Guildford City football ground is seen top left, Recreation Road sports ground at top centre, and the Woodbridge Road sports ground is on the far right. A suburban train crosses the bridge over the river and Walnut Tree Close as its takes the curve towards the station.

Flying high over Guildford soon after the cathedral was completed, but before the university began to spread over the north side of Stag Hill. Madrid Road is seen bottom left with Ridgemount forming a right angle in the centre of the picture. The land in between has now been filled in with housing.

The Cathedral of the Holy Spirit

The Cathedral of the Holy Spirit dominates the skyline, but many Guildfordians remember Stag Hill as it used to be for it was only in the 1930s that the building of the great church commenced. Guildford had separated from Winchester diocese in 1927 and Harold Greig was enthroned as the first bishop in Holy Trinity Church in the High Street. However, this church was considered to be too small and Lord Onslow of Clandon Park gave six acres of land on Stag Hill for what was to become only the fourth cathedral to be built since the Reformation and the first on a new site. This photograph, taken from The Mount, looks across to Stag Hill in 1936 when preparatory work had begun to drive concrete piles into the clay.

Roadmakers at work on construction of the main approach to the cathedral. The new bypass road can be seen in the background

Small boys and old men watch as the first of 778 concrete piles is steam-driven into the clay on Stag Hill on Wednesday, 8 July 1936. Older residents can still bring to mind the noise of the hammer banging down on the piles, each weighing five tons and 50ft in length, which reverberated around the town. Above left, the bishop, Dr J.V.Macmillan, addresses men from Trollope & Colls of Dorking who worked long hours to ensure that the cathedral had a solid foundation.

Bricks used in the building of the cathedral were made from the clay excavated from Stag Hill when the concrete piles were driven into the ground. The trilby-hatted workman has his back to one of the piles. In the background is the cross, made from timbers taken from *HMS Ganges*, which Bishop Greig unveiled on 19 April 1933.

22 July 1936. The foundation stone of Guildford Cathedral is laid by the Archbishop of Canterbury, the Rt Rev Cosmo Gordon Lang. The ceremony, held on a beautiful summer day, attracted 10,000 people. In the foreground, a boy can be seen perched on top of one of the concrete piles which had been driven into Stag Hill.

Craftsmen from a wide area were employed on building the cathedral. Here, a stonemason puts a large block of stone into place.

By November 1938, the building was taking shape – this photograph shows the children's chapel – but within a year Britain was at war with Germany and all activity on Stag Hill had ground to a halt. Work did not begin again until 1952.

Taking stock. The architect, Sir Edward Maufe (left), shows Bishop Macmillan around the unfinished cathedral in 1939.

The great Easter pilgrimage to the still unfinished cathedral in 1955. Below, the pilgrims in costume make their way over Farnham Road railway bridge on their way to Stag Hill. In the foreground, the roof of the roundhouse of the engine sheds; in the background, the three gasholders in the area of Bedford Road close to where the law courts now stand.

The Queen meets Sir Edward Maufe, cathedral architect, during a visit on 27 June 1957. Later, Sir Edward said the Queen had told him that the building was 'so serene and beautiful'. Below, members of the public, in their thousands, signed their names on bricks purchased for 2s 6d in the great push to complete the building. Bricks signed by the Queen and Prince Philip are displayed inside the cathedral.

George Reindorp, the last Bishop of Guildford to be enthroned in Holy Trinity Church in the town centre, was the bishop when the cathedral was consecrated on 17 May 1961, a quarter of a century after the foundation stone had been laid. Here, Bishop Reindorp is pictured with young Christians during a diocesan pilgrimage to Stag Hill on Easter Monday 1962.

The congregation is turned towards the great west door as Bishop Reindorp knocks for admission at the start of the service of consecration on 17 May 1961.

Guildford Cathedral has attracted millions of visitors since work began in 1936 but, apart from royalty, none more recognisable than Mother Teresa of Calcutta on 3 November 1970. To her left is the Dean, the Very Rev Tony Bridge.

The Golden Angel weather-vane on top of the cathedral.

Surrey Weekly Press

39th Year. Vol. XX XIX No. 1972 | Registered at the G.P.O. as a Newspaper | Friday, May 27, 1938 | Price ONE PENNY | By Post—2s. 3d. per quarter, 8s. 8d. per annum.

MAYOR LAYS FIRST BRICK OF CATHEDRAL

Stag Hill Ceremony Marred By Heavy Rain

Braving heavy rain, more than two hundred people climbed the slopes of Stag Hill on Wednesday afternoon to witness the fifth historic ceremony to be performed there—the laying of the first brick of the first part of the Cathedral Church of the Holy Spirit in Guildford by the First Citizen of the town, the Mayor (Alderman H. Gammon).

After laying the brick, the Mayor said that his feelings that afternoon were feelings of pride that, through the position he held, he was privileged to play some small part in a big undertaking that had been so well commenced.

BISHOP BLESSES BRICK

Education Committee Support School Libraries Proposal

"ZEAL AND FAITH"

RAIN AT LAST, BUT NO SPORTS

GODALMING TAXI-OWNERS OBJECT TO PROPOSED NEW SERVICE

GODALMING COUNCIL CRITICISED FOR MAKING CONCESSION TO TERRITORIAL-EMPLOYEES

Bungalows For Old-Age Pensioners

APPLICATIONS TO BE INVITED FROM GUILDFORD RESIDENTS

MISS A. C. MELLERISH

MR. T. L. LIVINGSTONE-LEARMOUTH

SURREY FOOTBALLERS IN BELGIUM

GUILDFORD MAN GETS DECREE

COUNCIL'S WARNING

BISHOP SAYS CHURCH PEOPLE ARE DOING COUNTRY'S BEST SOCIAL WORK

"REAL POWER HOUSE"

ANNIVERSARY SERVICE AT CHARTERHOUSE

CHURCH CENTRAL SCHOOLS

FINANCIAL STATEMENT

IMPS HOLD DANCE, RAMBLE AND TREASURE HUNT

Front page news: The *Surrey Weekly Press* of Friday, 27 May 1938, tells the story of the laying of the first brick at the cathedral by the mayor, Alderman H. Gammon.

Churches & Chapels

The tower of St Mary's Church in Quarry Street dates from the eleventh century which makes it the oldest building in the town. Other parts of the church date from the middle of the thirteenth century. Considerable restoration work took place in 1863 under the guidance of the architect Thomas Goodchild.

This is the St Nicholas Church, built in 1836, which replaced one dating from medieval times. It was so poorly built that it lasted only 39 years and was replaced by the present church at the bottom of the High Street.

Consecrated on 20 April 1876, the current St Nicolas Church is seen here in the early years of the century. To the front and left is John Moon & Sons, timber merchants. The whitewashed building which occupies this spot today had been used as a motor garage and offices before brewers Fuller, Smith & Turner, of Chiswick, transformed it into a pub in 1995 and gave it the appropriate name of The White House.

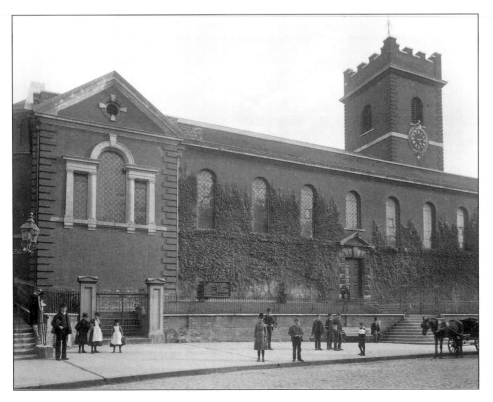

Ivy creeps up a large part of the north wall of Holy Trinity Church on a picture postcard which was posted in 1908. The clock shows it is nearly a quarter past five and the assembled crowd stands around as if waiting for something to happen. This scene today, if it were a weekday at least, would see the High Street gripped in the evening rush hour, and would anyone bother to stop and watch a photographer at work? Holy Trinity was built in 1763 as a replacement for a thirteenth-century church whose tower and steeple collapsed in 1740. When Guildford diocese was formed in 1927, Holy Trinity became the cathedral church until the consecration of the Cathedral of the Holy Spirit in 1961.

The Church of St John in Stoke Road, long before its modern Stirling Centre was added. The woman standing on the corner of Josephs Road is looking over the wall at the war memorial for the parish of Stoke-next-Guildford. The wall is still standing but the memorial has been resited on the opposite side of Stoke Road, at the entrance to the Lido and indoor bowls centre.

There was once a saying which went: Pretty Guildford, proud people, three churches, no steeple. And there were even more churches in the town by the time St Saviour's was built in Woodbridge Road, complete with its fine steeple. In fact, the church took nine years to build and in the final stages of completion, in the spring of 1906, two men risked life and limb in a contest to climb the 135ft spire. Former sailor Charles West, 63, was dared by a friend to climb the scaffolding of the three-quarters built steeple. This he did on a Saturday afternoon after the workmen had gone home. The following week, with more masonry added, another fellow eclipsed West's efforts. The news soon spread and West was determined to have the last say in the matter. He waited until the steeple was complete, and with only a day or so before the scaffolding was removed, made his second ascent – this time at night. A crowd gathered to watch him negotiate the 450 scaffold poles, and as they saw him touch the very top of the spire, by the light of the moon, they let out three cheers.

Christ Church in Waterden Road was consecrated in 1868 but the building work was not completed until the 1900s. Originally part of Stoke-next-Guildford parish, Christ Church became a parish in its own right in 1936. In 1962 it was redecorated to plans by Sir Edward Maufe, the architect of the cathedral, and has undergone restoration to the tune of £70,000 this year, with a further £50,000 spent on the organ.

The corrugated iron mission hall known as St Luke's Church, and its adjoining institute, stood towards the far end of Addison Road. When, in 1945, it was decided to change the name of the nearby Warren Road Hospital, it took its new name from this church, St Luke also being the patron saint of the medical profession.

All change at the bottom of North Street. This early 1970s view shows workmen demolishing the Methodist Church which had stood there since 1894. It had replaced an earlier place of worship built in 1844.

Guildford Park Road in the early years of the century showing the corrugated-iron Evangelical Gospel church.

Stoke Bridges from the towpath of the Wey Navigation with the landmark building of Stoke Mill standing out majestically on the right-hand side. A little weather-boarded chapel stands on what is now a very boggy island between the two bridges.

Emergency & Welfare Services

The fire station in North Street was built in 1872 and replaced an older building which was little more than a brick and wooden shed. Here, the brigade poses showing the full height of one of its ladders. The two arched entrances were altered at about the time motor-driven Dennis fire engines replaced the horse-drawn 'steamers'.

Moving on a few years, we see the fire station with the brigade showing off its fine Dennis fire engines.

A blaze broke out at Annie Pratt's furniture store in Woodbridge Road just after 1pm on Wednesday, 11 January 1911. The alarm was sounded and the fire brigade soon arrived with Foreman Reading in charge. Passers-by rescued some of the shop's stock, but most of it was destroyed along with the building. At one stage it was feared that the fire would spread next door to Pelham House, owned by Mr W.R.Handsell, the secretary of the Guildford Fire Brigade. However, with help from workers at the Friary Brewery, the brigade eventually put out the blaze.

Fire ripped through the building occupied by Record & Co's blouse shop in the High Street on the night of Sunday, 1 January 1922. A family sleeping in rooms above the shop were awakened by the smoke and flames and made a lucky escape in their nightclothes. Firemen tackled the blaze from the front and back of the shop. Dennis Bros' own brigade was also called on to help. Damage to the tune of £20,000 was done to the building, which stood near the Cornmarket. The adjoining Lipton's shop was also damaged. The gabled buildings dated from the sixteenth century and were later rebuilt in almost exactly the same style.

The Borough Police Station in North Street, now occupied by a Laura Ashley shop.

PC Tyrell (left), PC Henley (centre) and PC Harry Bird (right) were members of Guildford Borough Police Force, whose first accommodation was in a cottage at 1 Tunsgate. It moved to the new station in North Street in 1892, when the population of Guildford was 14,000.

The badge of the Guildford Borough Police force from 1836 until its dissolution in 1947.

Guildford Borough Police force in 1933 pictured in front of the war memorial in the Castle Grounds. In the middle of the front row are the Mayor of Guildford, Alderman William Harvey, and the town clerk, Mr C.H. Wood. To the mayor's left is Walter Oliver, Chief Constable of Guildford from 1929 until 1943 when the borough force temporarily merged with Surrey Constabulary, the amalgamation becoming permanent four years later. This was the second time the forces had amalgamated. Back in 1851, soon after Surrey Constabulary had been established, the two came together but three years later the borough force was reconstituted after a disagreement over police stations.

This informal photograph of Surrey police officers formed part of the constabulary's Christmas card, probably just after the end of World War One. It was taken outside the then police headquarters in Woodbridge Road. The Chief Constable of Surrey from 1899 to 1930, Capt Mowbray Sant, is in the foreground, with the cane. Capt Sant became what has been termed the 'arch-enemy' of the early Automobile Association patrols, and he challenged the AA to show that the scouts were not 'a deliberate interference with the duties of my constables and with my duties as Chief Constable of Surrey'.

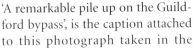

'A remarkable pile up on the Guildford bypass', is the caption attached to this photograph taken in the mid-1930s by the late Tom Roberts (pictured), who was then a detective sergeant with Surrey Constabulary. The driver of the car at the top of the pile was ex-Chief Inspector Gooch, who had recently retired from the Metropolitan Police where he had been head of the flying squad. Mr Gooch died from the injuries he received. Mr Roberts joined the police force on Boxing Day 1925 and was a detective superintendent within 17 years. As a young constable he took photography lessons and was put in charge of developing the new photographic department to serve the whole county. This led to him becoming a pioneer of forensic science which was to see him play an important role in solving many Surrey murder cases in the 1930s and 1940s. Tom Roberts left the police service on secondment to the War Office in the early 1950s, and on retirement in 1969 he became an industrial security consultant. He died in December 1989, aged 84.

The Chief Constable of Guildford, Mr W.V. Nicholas, died in May 1929, and here his funeral procession moves along Portsmouth Road and begins to turn into the then entrance to The Mount cemetery. Mr Nicholas had headed the Guildford force for 20 years, since moving from Oxford, where he had been deputy chief constable. His starting salary in Guildford was £180 a year. His uniform, residence and fuel were supplied by the corporation. The force, which by then numbered 30, had been formed at a watch committee meeting on Friday, 15 January 1836, following the passing of the Municipal Corporation Act the previous year. The first constable to be appointed in Guildford was Charles Mandeville, who wore a stove-pipe hat and a uniform with the number 1 on its collar. Walter Oliver, who succeeded Mr Nicholas, was Guildford's last chief constable, retiring in 1943 when the borough force began its amalgamation with Surrey Constabulary.

Ambulancemen line up beside their vehicles outside the St John Ambulance Brigade headquarters in Leas Road in 1952. The ambulances were supplied by F.G.Barnes and Sons Ltd, then based on the A3 at Ladymead.

The original Royal Surrey County Hospital was opened in April 1866 in Farnham Road. The cost of the building, £17,000, had been raised by public subscription. It replaced the Guildford Dispensary which had opened only some seven years earlier in Quarry Street. The Royal Surrey was designed as a general hospital serving not only the town, but the whole county. It was dedicated to the memory of the late Prince Albert and was opened with 60 beds. Until 1928 it was run along the lines of a charity for the sick poor. Then, until the National Health Service came into being in 1948, the hospital operated under a contributory scheme known as the West Surrey and Aldershot Hospitals League.

The nurses home at the Royal Surrey County Hospital in Farnham Road pictured soon after it was built in 1908. This was designed by the Guildford architect Edward Lunn.

The Guildford Union Workhouse was opened in 1838 in Union Lane (Warren Road since 1904). An infirmary was added in 1896 for the sick poor of the town. It was used as a military hospital during World War One when this photograph was taken. Known as Warren Road Hospital from 1930 to 1945, it was then renamed St Luke's Hospital. In latter years the site also became a centre for radiotherapy and housed the Guildford School of Nursing, a midwifery school and a school of radiography. The buildings seen in this picture were pulled down in 1965.

A group of half a dozen or so buildings formed the Woodbridge Isolation Hospital which bordered the railway line near the Dennis works. Note the large ventilation units on the roof of each block.

The isolation hospital was designed by Henry Peak and was used from the last decades of the nineteenth century until 1940. These rare images have been copied from photographs pasted into his personal diaries. Mr Peak (1832-1914) was born in Clerkenwell and came to Guildford in 1851 as assistant to Mr W.Moss, architect and surveyor. Thirty years later he joined Edward Lunn in a partnership that was to last two decades, until his retirement, and which resulted in much important and lasting work in the town. Mr Peak was also borough surveyor for 27 years and worked on the development of Charlotteville, with Dr Sells; the Markenfield estate, with William Wells, farmer and brickmaker; and buildings in Stoughton.

The superintendent's house at the Woodbridge Isolation Hospital. Patients with infectious diseases such as typhoid, scarlet fever and diphtheria were treated here. The hospital was administered by a local government board. It had its own ambulance. The board also ran a second isolation hospital on Whitmoor Common at Worplesdon, from 1900 to 1931, which cared for smallpox patients.

The Pub Bombings

Surrey Daily Advertiser
AND GUILDFORD TIMES

Monday Noon to Tuesday Noon (October 7th/8th, 1974)

YOUR LOCAL DAILY FAMILY NEWSPAPER

FREE

Price 3p 13093

PLANNED MURDER

Bomb blast toll

Picture: John Carter

World-wide net for killers

POLICE are casting a world-wide net for the mass-murderers who planted bombs in two Guildford public houses on Saturday. By now the bombers could be anywhere — but they may still be in the area.

'I think they've killed my Mum and Dad...'

Royal message

Injury latest

Distress appeal

Continued on page 11

Continued page 10.

Continued page 1

More on the explosions on pages 3, 9, 10, 11, 12.

Arguably the most dramatic front page in the 134 years of the *Surrey Advertiser*. The newspaper had recently converted to daily publication when the pub bombers struck in Guildford on Saturday, 5 October 1974. This was the issue of Monday, 7 October.

The immediate aftermath of Guildford's night of terror when the IRA bombed two town centre pubs on Saturday, 5 October 1974. Five people died and 65 were injured when a bomb exploded inside the Horse and Groom in North Street. The pub was frequented on Saturday nights by soldiers stationed at Aldershot and Pirbright who came to Guildford in search of entertainment.

A closer view of the twisted façade of the North Street pub. There had been a hostelry on the site since the early nineteenth century.

Police and firemen on duty outside the wreckage of the Horse and Groom, shortly after the bomb went off at 8.50pm.

The morning after Guildford's black Saturday, and pedestrians, with their own private thoughts, stand and look at the scene of the senseless violence. The Horse and Groom reopened after a £50,000 refit, and in time its name was changed to Grooms, but it never recovered from that awful night in 1974 and has been closed for some years.

Damage to the Seven Stars in Swan Lane was not so extensive, and there was no loss of life. It reopened, briefly, in April 1975, and is now an off-licence.

The Home Secretary, Roy (now Lord) Jenkins, visited the town to inspect the damage caused by the bombers. He is pictured approaching the Seven Stars in Swan Lane with, on the left, the Chief Constable of Surrey, Peter Matthews, and the head of Scotland Yard's bomb squad, Commander Robert Huntley.

The MP for Guildford, David (now Lord) Howell, a former Northern Ireland minister, and the Chief Constable, Peter Matthews (later knighted) in Swan Lane on the night of the bombings.

The first appearance by one of the four people who were eventually charged with the Guildford pub bombings took place on Monday, 2 December 2, 1974, at the magistrates' court in Ward Street, just round the corner from the bombed Horse and Groom. Paul Hill, Gerard Conlon, Patrick Armstrong and Carole Richardson were subsequently found guilty at the Old Bailey and given life sentences. They always protested their innocence, became known as the Guildford Four and, in October 1989, were released from prison when appeal court judges found there were doubts about their convictions. Following that, three Surrey police officers were cleared of fabricating evidence and, in July 1994, the then chief constable, David Williams, announced that the force was finally able to close the book on Guildford's most infamous date in history.

Floods & Storms

The power of nature: The aftermath of the floods of 15 February 1900, when timber from Moon's yard was hurled by the fast-flowing river into the town bridge. This, combined with the sheer force of the water, made the old bridge crumble and collapse. Two years later a new bridge was opened. Crooke's Brewery can be seen in the background.

On the evening of 2 August 1906, 'a thunderstorm of tremendous violence broke over the town and district of Guildford', reported the *Surrey Times*, adding: 'The brilliant and almost continuous flashes of lightning and terrific peals of thunder were accompanied by a perfect tornado of wind, which caused great damage to all parts of the town.' Ruth Blunden, 23, and 14-year-old Charles Voice lost their lives when the trees which they were sheltering under were blown down at Woodbridge Avenue, close to the junction with Stocton Road. The picture shows the extent of the damage near the scene where Miss Blunden was rescued from the fallen branches. At the inquest into her death, it was reported that she was carried on a stretcher to the Royal Surrey County Hospital in Farnham Road. PC Frederick Laurence told the jury that on the way she groaned very much. She was still alive when they passed the Elm Tree Tavern, but he heard no more groaning after they reached Bridge Street.

The photographer, Dann of Redhill, raced to Guildford the day after the 1906 great storm and recorded a number of views of the damage. These were soon reproduced as picture postcards. Here, workmen can be seen amid a fallen tree in Josephs Road. The *Surrey Times* issued a special publication for one halfpenny reprinted from its edition of 4 August. It also offered picture postcards at a penny each of the scenes in Woodbridge Avenue, the Town Bridge and a pair of cottages along Shalford Road, where a bedridden Mr J.Cooper, 78, had a lucky escape when a large fir tree crashed through the roof of his home.

With the storm safely past, crowds flocked to see the damage to the Town Bridge. On the opposite side of the river can be seen rowing boats belonging to Harry How who had a tea room on the river frontage. Two of his hire boats were submerged.

This close-up view shows the damage to the Town Bridge. It was hit by a large elm tree which had stood on the west side of the river by Moon's timber yard. In reporting the incident, the *Surrey Times* said that the falling tree 'came into contact with the parapet of the bridge, and for a distance of some three or four yards the steel was smashed to atoms'.

A superb view of Woodbridge Road, looking towards the town. This is another of Dann of Redhill's work taken after the 1906 storm. There is a wealth of detail here from the horse-drawn carriages to the clothes of the children. One of the shops is being repaired. Part of the zinc roof of the cattle market opposite (not in view) was ripped off during the height of the storm and crashed into the sub-post office and greengrocer's shop.

Deep, drifting snow, up to 15ft in places, on the Hog's Back during Christmas 1927 made the road practically impassable. Men struggle to free a Lymposs & Smee Dairy delivery van which had been stuck for three days. The old style milk churns can just be seen inside the vehicle.

Deep floodwater at the bottom of the High Street. This was on 3 January 1928, after the town had been covered by 1ft of snow at Christmas. On New Year's Day there was a slight rise in temperature, followed by heavy rain the following day which resulted in the floods on the third day of January. The Alvis car is on the west side of the Town Bridge. Opposite St Nicolas Church (right) is the Connaught Family and Commercial Hotel which was demolished in 1942 to make room for the Farnham Road bus station, now a car park. The unlicensed Connaught had previously been the home of the Crooke family, whose brewery was set back behind the house and backing on to the river. Crooke's Brewery, which owned many pubs in the town and district, was taken over by Hodgsons Kingston Brewery Co in 1929. Fourteen years later Hodgsons was sold to Courage Barclay and Simonds, the forerunner of Courage.

Friary Street was always badly affected when Guildford flooded. Here, on 3 January 1928, the street was under its customary several inches of muddy water.

All manner of debris floats on the January 1928 floodwaters. As always, a sizeable crowd has gathered at the bottom of the High Street.

Once again the River Wey has burst its banks, this time in June 1936. The motorcyclist is trying his luck in Onslow Street. Behind him a man leads a horse and cart. Note the Woodbridge Press building in the background, now part of a nightclub, which is where the *Surrey Times* was printed for many years.

After a heavy rainfall it always seemed to flood at Woodbridge Meadows opposite the Co-op Dairy. The number 20 bus to Aldershot via Rydes Hill seems to be making good progress, though. This undated picture looks to have been taken during the 1950s when any structure that could take an advertisement was usually seized upon. The Haslemere Motor Co, advertising on both the bus and the bridge, was based at the Morris Depot on the corner of Ladymead and Woodbridge Road.

On Saturday night, 14 September 1968, it began raining. There was a torrential downpour throughout Sunday and, by Monday, the River Wey had burst its banks and the bottom of the High Street was under six feet of water. The sun shone again that day, bringing out hundreds of onlookers standing on the 'new banks' of the river to see what nature had delivered.

At his home in Guildford, amateur meteorologist Dennis Mullen recorded 3.75 inches of rain on Sunday, 15 September 1968, while a spokesman for the West Surrey Water Board described the floods as a disaster which happened only once in a thousand years. The extent of the flooding can clearly be seen here at the old town mill in front of the Yvonne Arnaud Theatre in Millbrook.

A watery view from the upper floors of Bridge House. The River Wey is in the foreground and the marooned vehicles are in Bedford Road. Guildford Laundry occupied a site in Laundry Road, near its junction with Bedford Road and roughly where the borough car park offices are today.

Inside the control room at the County Police HQ at Mount Browne, Guildford, on the Tuesday after the weekend deluge. The chief constable, Peter Matthews, is standing behind the desk, and a military liaison officer, Major Stuart James Symonds, Royal Engineers, is on the right. Across Surrey thousands of people were forced to leave their homes, while cinemas, theatres, factories and schools were closed, along with railway lines where bridges were damaged. Electricity supplies were cut and in the aftermath there was a real fear that there would be a shortage of drinking water. Up to 300 people were evacuated from their homes in Guildford, many of them spending the Sunday night at the Sandfield Terrace Drill Hall, with the WRVS making sure everyone was as comfortable as possible.

Mopping up began on the Tuesday. The Yvonne Arnaud Theatre suffered badly although, as the floodwaters rose the previous day, scenery for its latest production was moved to safety. A rowing boat was used to make trips between a wall above the water level and the stage door. The theatre did not reopen for several weeks.

Wellington boots were the order of the day as cleaning up began at the Seeboard electricity store in Millbrook after the 1968 floodwaters had receded. Guildford's municipal offices became the co-ordinating centre for all flood relief operations. The council wrote to everyone affected, asking for full details of the damage, loss and extent of insurance cover.

Homes along Walnut Tree Close were badly affected by the floods. But soon everyone was mucking in together to help out. Seen here are guides and scouts who lent a hand with their buckets and mops.

The big clean-up goes on at the Yvonne Arnaud Theatre. Nearby, the basement of Plummers store (now Debenhams) in Millbrook was flooded with much stock ruined. By the Monday lunchtime the water level had risen to ground floor levels. The store placed an advertisement in that weekend's *Surrey Advertiser* telling customers it would remain closed while salvage operations were in progress. Subsequent river improvements have kept Guildford free of flooding for 30 years.

On the River Wey

The origins of the Wey Navigation can be traced back as far as 1635 when Sir Richard Weston, of Sutton Place, constructed a lock on the river at Stoke. His plan to make the river navigable as far as the Thames was halted by the Civil War, but in 1653 the work, featuring 12 locks, was completed. Sir Richard did not live to see his dream fulfilled, but his son George certainly felt the backlash of the whole scheme. In fact, the Weston family suffered severe financial difficulties over it. However, after 1671, when a body of governing trustees was appointed, the navigation at last began to prosper. This 1962 picture shows the offices of the Wey Navigation, which were off Friary Street. All that remains on the site today is the three-ton treadwheel crane building.

For many years the Stevens family were connected with the river, and from 1930 to 1965 Harry Stevens owned the Navigation. His great-grandfather had first worked at Thames Lock, Weybridge, in 1820. Barges were built at Dapdune Wharf in Guildford, and this picture shows the launching of a barge in the early 1930s. The barge had not yet been fully fitted out and the rudder was still to be added.

Members of the Stevens family were obviously keen cricketers in Victorian times. The picture was taken by the Surrey Photo Company of 32 High Street, Guildford.

Another family connected with the Wey Navigation were the Edwards who built the barges. Each barge would take between 18 months and two years to build with three people employed to do the work.

Most barges on the Wey would have been horse-drawn. However, as this Victorian picture shows, sailing barges could also be found on the river, as seen here at Millmead.

And of course pleasure craft used the river as well. The man with the beard and straw boater is William Stevens III, pictured with his wife Kate and their son Harry, with his arm around the post. Notice the coloured glass night lights strung up along the boat.

Here is another outing photographed on 3 June 1908, at Stoke Lock and subsequently published as a picture postcard. It is the event of the GWNC picnic, but what this organisation represented is not known. The postcard was sent to a Miss P.Dean at Cranleigh School on 28 July of that year, by a person called Gertie, who wrote saying that she was one of the women pictured in the boat but had not the time to write a letter as she was very busy.

Stoke Lock in August 1952 and the gates are being opened to let one of Stevens's barges through.

The River Wey meandering through the countryside at Woodbridge Meadows at the turn of the century. This is the old brick-built Wood Bridge, replaced in 1913. On the far left is where the Post Office sorting depot is today and in the distance a row of cottages in Weyside Road, at that time called Cemetery Road, can just be made out.

A 1966 view of the Guildford wharf off Friary Street. All this was demolished to make way for the shops of the modern precinct.

The Wey Navigation was extended upstream to Godalming after 1760. Goods soon being carried included grain, as well as gunpowder from the mills at Chilworth. This is Tumbling Bay at Millmead, pictured at the end of the nineteenth century.

The river has frozen over in this picture showing the Jolly Farmer public house and Leroy's Boathouse in the harsh winter of 1963. Marion Smailes, pictured here, and her husband, Leslie, owned and operated Leroy's from 1961 to 1974.

And now the water has gone! The navigation at Millmead sometime during the early 1970s when it was temporarily drained for maintenance.

The boathouse near the Jolly Farmer has for many years been a focal point for activity on the river. In about 1900, according to the sign board, it was the headquarters of the Guildford Swimming Club and the local branch of the Life Saving Society. Today, it is the still a place where rowing boats can be hired in the summer months and the embarkation point for narrow boat holidays. It is also the base of the pleasure boat, the *Alfred Leroy*.

A short way upstream from Millmead, on a bend of the river, there was once a lime wharf owned by George Davis. Chalk was quarried from a nearby pit now renamed The Great Quarry.

The little girl's smock dress is really the only giveaway to say that this photograph was taken before World War One. The lane leading down from St Catherine's to the ferry crossing on the river was much the same then as it is today.

The ferry crossing at St Catherine's seen in the closing years of the last century. The last ferry operated in 1963 and now there is a footbridge to take travellers over the river to Shalford Park. The National Trust is responsible for the care and maintenance of the River Wey Navigation, which flows from Godalming to Weybridge. At its offices at Dapdune Wharf, Guildford, there is an information centre and a river bus service operates on certain days of the week. The trust is active in protecting the 20-mile length of navigation from damage, while highlighting the decline of farming and increased recreational use as the main pressures on the riverside environment.

Transport

The engine sheds in April 1965. A photograph that evokes all the history and passion of steam locomotives. Long since demolished, memories of the great days of railway travel on the London to Portsmouth line have all but faded. The site remained empty for many years before the borough council, faced with the prospect of more and more vehicles squeezing the life out of the town centre, opened a cleverly designed multi-storey car park on the vacant space.

The ever faithful taxis wait at the entrance of the railway station for incoming trains – only here they are horse drawn. This 1900s view shows the London & South Western Railway station buildings which were largely constructed in the 1880s. Note the rather ornate canopy or porte-cochere. In latter years, many of the station buildings had become dilapidated and the entrance to the booking hall and platforms had been changed. They were finally pulled down in 1988 to make way for a new station and forecourt.

Up from Pompey! Seen at Guildford station in the 1920s, this former London & South Western Railway class N15 4-6-0 locomotive, No.753, was the latest thing when acquired by the newly-formed Southern Railway in 1923. In 1937 the first electric trains ran between London Waterloo and Portsmouth, via Guildford.

Once upon a time every schoolboy (and adult) trainspotter's dream was to get a good look around a loco shed. Rarely used or redundant engines lurking in the shadows would be an excellent 'cop' and proudly crossed off in the spotter's loco book. This photograph of the sheds, codenamed 70C in BR days, was taken before nationalisation in 1948. Here, it is full of Southern Railway locos. In the centre is a small 'saddle tank' which would have acted as a pilot pulling and pushing the 'dead' – out of steam – locos, on and off the turntable.

A London & South Western Railway M7 tank engine trundles over the bridge at Woodbridge Hill with a London-bound train in the early 1900s. How different this scene appears today. In 1995, there was the opportunity to stand at the same spot and photograph a similar class of locomotive, also running bunker first in the same direction, hauling a steam special. The result: A picture that did not have anywhere near as much charm as this one. Nowadays, the road is lined with parked cars and an ugly concrete footbridge partially obscures the railway embankment.

Shortly before midnight on 9 February 1911, a traction engine and trailer passing through Guildford en route to Southampton overturned in Epsom Road, killing one of its three occupants. The *Surrey Advertiser* of 13 February, reporting the inquest into the death of David Boxall, 65, of Epsom, said that an eyewitness saw the traction engine careering out of control at 12mph. The driver, William Collins, told the inquest that he tried to put the engine into reverse gear when he realised how steep the road was, but the gear pin fell out and he lost control of the vehicle. A verdict of accidental death was returned.

A busy scene at the Farnham Road bus station believed to be in the late 1940s. Most of the people are hurrying across the town bridge towards the High Street. Bus companies operating in and out of Guildford in those days included the Aldershot & District Traction Company, Safeguard, Tillingbourne and the Yellow Bus Company.

Made in Guildford: This Aldershot & District Traction Company Dennis bus was probably built on a chassis dating from the time of World War One. It is pictured in the station yard in the early 1920s and was bound for Ripley, according to its destination board. It is standing beside a wagon of the Great Northern Railway Company.

One of the most sensational fatalities on the Guildford bypass occurred on the morning of Friday, 22 January 1959, when the world motor-racing champion, Mike Hawthorn, was killed instantly as his 3.4-litre Jaguar left the road just south of the cathedral. Hawthorn, who was known as the Farnham Flyer, was driving from his home to London, where he was due to collect yet another prestigious award following his Formula One success over pre-season favourite Stirling Moss. The idol of a generation of impressionable boys, the blond-haired, bow-tied Hawthorn thrilled motor-racing fans throughout the 1950s, culminating in his world crown in a Ferrari in 1958. His death, only a matter of weeks later, shook the sporting world to its foundations. The aerial view, taken shortly after the accident, shows a still quite rural scene at Stag Hill. The road is dual carriageway but without a central reservation. The arrows demonstrate Hawthorn's path and the cross marks the spot, beside the opposite carriageway, where his car crashed into a tree. Soon after the accident, people began to arrive at the scene to leave flowers to the memory of the man who many Guildfordians remembered as an apprentice with Dennis Brothers just after World War Two. Hawthorn's funeral service in Farnham brought his home town to a standstill. There were floral tributes from around the world, many of them from the greatest names in motor sport, and for weeks afterwards still shocked members of the public made their way to his grave in Farnham cemetery to pay their last respects.

Here we see the newly-completed Wood Bridge spanning the River Wey in 1913. Through the centre of the arch can be seen one of the pillars of the previous bridge. Another bridge has now been built alongside to cope with the increasing traffic on the A3.

The premises of F.G.Barnes and Sons Ltd, one of Guildford's major motor dealers, were built at Ladymead in 1936 to coincide with the opening of the bypass. The company was first to apply to Guildford council to release land at Slyfield for industrial purposes, and moved to its present headquarters in Moorfield Road in 1971. The road at Ladymead was widened in 1962 and the Barnes site is now the car park for a B & Q store.

A street-cleaning machine shortly after World War One. Made by F.G.Barnes in Godalming, it was both a tar spraying and brushing contraption. The winch and gantry hoisted tar barrels above the tank. Hot tar was collected from the gas works and then reheated in the machine by coils from the steam traction engine.

A Military Presence – War & Remembrance

The Queen's Regiment has been linked to Guildford for many years, but its origins go back to 1661 when Charles II gave orders for the raising of a horse and foot infantry to garrison Tangier. It changed its name to The Queen's Regiment in 1684 and served in places such as Ireland, Spain, India and Afghanistan. In October 1876 it transferred to new barracks built at Stoughton on the outskirts of Guildford. It became the Queen's Royal West Surrey Regiment in 1881 and this view shows the impressive keep and officers' mess in about 1900.

Stoughton Barracks was just two years old when this photograph was taken of Lt Pink and officers of the 2nd Surrey Militia in 1878.

A Francis Frith picture postcard view of the parade ground at Stoughton Barracks with the Third Battalion of the Queen's Royal West Surrey Regiment on parade. Local historians are fortunate to have such a good record of the barracks and Stoughton at the turn of the century, as a number of postcard publishers produced views. These must have been popular with the young soldiers who sent them to family and friends showing them what their 'new home' was like.

The date is 1 June 1910, and members of the corporals' depot of The Queen's Royal Regiment are pictured just prior to setting off from Stoughton Barracks for their annual outing to the Derby. Presumably, the horse-drawn bus would have taken them to Guildford railway station where they would have boarded a train to Epsom. Note the recruiting posters outside the barracks' entrance.

Another view of the keep at Stoughton Barracks with a lone sergeant watching out for any movements of personnel. A 1952 booklet aimed at recruits states that a young regular on arriving at the depot 'will become part of the intake machine. Certain documents will be prepared and information given to him. He will then draw his bedding from the store and be issued with his uniform and equipment'. The weekly pay for a young private at this time was 49 shillings (£2.45) rising to 178 shillings and sixpence (£35.72) for a warrant officer with eight years' experience.

At the far end of Stoughton Barracks there was a sports field complete with its own pavilion. The crowd of soldiers in this 1933 photograph certainly seem pleased with the cricketer with the bat.

Guildford Castle Grounds once displayed this gun which was a souvenir from the Boer War.

A banquet in the Drill Hall in Sandfield Terrace was attended by nearly 1,000 officers and men of The Queen's (Royal West Surrey) Regiment. It took place on Saturday, 8 October 1904 and included soldiers of the 2nd Battalion stationed at Shorncliffe in Kent. It marked the unveiling of five memorials in Holy Trinity Church to those who died in the Boer War. The cost of the memorials was raised by public subscription in a campaign led by the Lord Lieutenant of Surrey, Viscount Midleton of Peper Harow, who unveiled the tablet dedicated to the 12 men of the 3rd Battalion who lost their lives. The regimental colonel unveiled the other major memorial which recorded the names of the 139 men of the 2nd Battalion who fell during the South African War. On this sombre day, the congregation was reminded of the October Friday five years earlier when the regiment embarked on the *Yorkshire* at Southampton and headed for the theatre of war. The men were laughing and joking; soon many of them were to be mown down and their bones left on that foreign soil. Lord Midleton attended the banquet, along with the Colonel of the Regiment, Lt Gen Sir Thomas Kelly-Kenny.

A wet High Street on 4 October 1913, and a large gathering of soldiers and townsfolk at the unveiling ceremony of a window in the chapel at Holy Trinity Church dedicated to The Queen's (Royal West Surrey) Regiment. The occasion marked the 250th anniversary of the raising of the regiment. Between 600 and 700 soldiers were present, including 400 from the 1st Battalion, who came by train from their barracks at Bordon. Also present were 100 soldiers based at Stoughton and another 100 territorials. The 2nd Battalion was serving abroad.

Off to the front: Troops march towards the railway station at the beginning of World War One in August 1914. This picture was issued as a postcard and was posted on 8 September of that year. It is proof of the large crowds which gathered to see off 'those brave young lads'.

The newly-built County School for Girls in Farnham Road had not welcomed its first pupils before it was commandeered in November 1914 as a Red Cross annexe attached to the Royal Surrey County Hospital on the other side of the road.

This postcard view shows a World War One tank which was presented to the town in 1919 in appreciation of Guildford's war savings achievements. It is seen here near to London Road railway station. It then remained at the bottom of North Street until 1923. Tanks were first introduced on the Somme in 1916 and, although unreliable at times, their sheer presence and power helped the Allies win the war against Germany.

A competition was held to design the memorial to those people from Guildford who died in World War One. Four local architects entered, and the judge, the distinguished architect, Sir Edwin Lutyens, chose the design submitted by Frederick Hodgson. The memorial was erected in 1920 and includes nearly 500 names of the dead from World War One. It was with some embarrassment that the names of more than 200 men and women from Guildford who fell in World War Two were only added to the memorial in November 1995.

For security reasons few picture postcards were produced during World War Two. However, there was the odd exception. This one carries a rallying call from Prime Minister Winston Churchill to the citizens of the borough with the classic view of the Guildhall. How could Guildfordians afford to let Jerry take this away from them?

The sign says it all: The Guildhall was without its famous clock for much of World War Two. It is believed it was taken to the crypt of the partially-built cathedral for safe keeping.

This rare wartime picture of Addison Road was published in the *Surrey Advertiser* on 17 May 1941. For security reasons the caption read: 'A street in a Home County residential suburb after bombs had been dropped by a German night raider. A large number of houses were more or less damaged.' The bomb fell in the back gardens between Cline Road and Addison Road, killing a man who was looking out of a window of a house in Cline Road. One house was destroyed. A Mr and Mrs Hill, their son and daughter and their two grandchildren were rescued alive from the rubble. The people whose homes were affected were offered alternative temporary accommodation at the Drill Hall in Sandfield Terrace.

There were many Home Guard units formed in and around Guildford during World War Two. Here, a platoon is pictured in front of the cathedral. You can just see the butt of a rifle which has been placed by the boarded-up doorway on the left. Perhaps these men were entrusted to guard the Guildhall clock and the rest of the borough's plate and regalia which allegedly were stored there.

The war's over: A street party in Ardmore Avenue, off Manor Road, Stoughton, to celebrate VE day in June 1945. The two boys on the left later became prominent borough councillors – Ralph Jordan and Bernard Parke.

YOU CAN SAVE MONEY

Do you ever stop to think of how much you would save if you bought a Cycle? Think of the money spent on bus and train fares, to say nothing of the time wasted.

YOU WILL SAVE MONEY

If you buy your Cycle from Pascalls, the Leading Cycle Agents in your district. Official Stockists for

B.S.A., ROYAL ENFIELD, ELSWICK, SCOTT, TRIUMPH, ETC.

EPascall (GUILDFORD) LTD

CORNER OF WOODBRIDGE ROAD AND NORTH STREET, GUILDFORD. Phone 255.

"GARDENS AT WAR"

Colour Films in support of the " Dig for Victory " Campaign will be shown at—

The Guildhall, GUILDFORD

On Tuesday, November 25th At 7.0 p.m.

Chairman :
HIS WORSHIP THE MAYOR

Speaker :
S. W. CHEVELEY, M.Sc.

ADMISSION FREE

Come and bring your friends.

MINISTRY OF SUPPLY

WANTED URGENTLY !

BY

Our Fighting Services

BINOCULARS

PUT YOUR PAIR ON ACTIVE SERVICE, NOW !

We are Authorised
:: Collectors. ::

JOHN HARWOOD
CONSULTING OPTICIAN
F.B.O.A. · (*HONOURS*)
 77 HIGH ST GUILDFORD

TELEPHONE 650.

THE GUILDFORD & DISTRICT CO-OPERATIVE SOCIETY LTD

The Hallmark of Value

THE CO-OP
RENDERS

'HOME' SERVICE

WHICH IS APPRECIATED

BY ALL WHO SERVE
ON THE

HOME FRONT

BEST VALUE, LOWEST PRICES, DIVIDEND TO MEMBERS.

KILL THAT RAT!

IT'S DOING HITLER'S WORK

Here in Britain is an enemy army of Rats living on us, devouring huge quantities of food, every ounce of which is precious in war time. Kill these pests now and stop this waste.

Rats are filthy, disease-carrying vermin. They haunt sewers, cess-pools, garbage dumps — wherever rotting refuse lies — there are the Rats. From wallowing in un-mentionable filth, these pests invade our larders, our food shops, our warehouses, gnawing and pawing and wasting food. Kill them now !

TRAP 'EM POISON 'EM GAS 'EM HUNT 'EM !

ASK FOR A LEAFLET
from your Local Authority. There is one for householders, another for factory owners and retailers, another for farmers and landowners. This Leaflet gives clear directions about the easiest ways to prevent and destroy Rats. Everyone can help.

Old Newspapers AND Magazines Bought

The "Surrey Advertiser" will buy your old Newspapers for cash. The price, which is controlled by the Ministry of Supply, is now

1d. for 3lb.

DELIVERED TO THE "SURREY ADVERTISER" OFFICE.

NOT FRIDAYS OR SATURDAYS

● Bundles should be securely tied with string and consist of OLD NEWSPAPERS ONLY. MAGAZINES AND PERIODICALS separately bundled

4 lb. for 1d.

SPOT CASH

"Surrey Advertiser" Office, Guildford.

A selection of wartime advertisements from the *Surrey Advertiser* of 1941.

On 29 September 1945, the Queen's Regiment was honoured with the privilege of 'marching through the streets of Guildford on all occasions with bayonets fixed, colours flying and bands playing'. The Mayor, Alderman Wykeham Price, in addressing the parade, said it was one of the greatest days the town had ever known. A march took place down the High Street, passing the mayor who stood at the Guildhall. Detachments from all battalions of the regiment were involved, including representatives from *HMS Excellent*. After a lunch for 200 guests at the Borough Hall, there was a football match between the regiment and *HMS Excellent*. The Queen's won 6-2. The Guildhall clock is still absent, although a smaller clock can be seen on the side of the balcony.

When men of the 8th Battalion, East Surrey Regiment, went 'over the top' at the Battle of the Somme in 1916 they kicked footballs before them towards the enemy lines which they successfully reached. This one, being held by Richard Ford, former police inspector who became curator of the Queen's Royal Surrey Regiment Museum at Clandon Park, was kicked by Capt W.P.Nevill, officer commanding B Company, on 1 July 1916 at Montauban Ridge. Entry to the museum is free of charge and its opening hours are the same as that of Clandon Park.

And the Queen's march past the Guildhall again. This time on 28 April 1960, when the regiment was presented with the Freedom of the Borough.

Time For Recreation

Fancy dress was worn on the day in 1909 when these people lined up for their photograph at the roller skating rink in Woodbridge Road. The rink was run as a sideline business by the Guildford architect Frederick Hodgson and a local solicitor by the name of Philpotts. It accommodated 150 skaters and they skated around on a floor of solid rock-maple. The building was erected by H.Brand to a design by Mr Hodgson and a Mr Symmonds. The roof was the responsibility of David Rowell & Co of London. The *Surrey Advertiser* reported in March 1910 that a music and dancing licence for the rink, which was behind Pelham House, had been granted between the hours of 10am and 10.30pm Monday to Saturday. The attraction was short-lived, however, and with the death of Edward VII, later in 1910, Guildfordians went into a state of mourning, and attendances fell away. There was also the growing threat of war and Pelham House rink did not recover its popularity.

The building which replaced the roller skating rink was also designed by Mr Hodgson and built in 1922 as the Cinema, seen here soon after it was opened. It later became the Guildford Cinema, with the Cinema Café next door. In later years it became the Astor and then Studios 1 and 2. After standing empty for some years, the building was refurbished in the early 1990s and became a nightspot.

A view of the interior of The Cinema in Woodbridge Road taken in the 1920s. Note the ornate decorations and pictures on the walls.

A triple bill of The Lorch Family, Mabel Costello and Will Brockton are providing the entertainment of the music hall fashion at the Theatre Royal on the corner of North Street and Commercial Road. Perhaps the stars of the show are the ones grouped in the middle of the picture.

A rarely-seen portrait of the young Yvonne Arnaud. The actress had supported Guildford's North Street Theatre and, in 1958, spent the last months of her life in the town. As a fitting tribute, the new theatre, when opened in 1965 was named after her. There is a memorial to her in the churchyard at St Martha's near Chilworth.

Come on in, you'll be amazed at what you might see. The early days of cinema at Guildford with the Picture Palace in Onslow Street. The building has remained an entertainment venue to this day. In the 1960s it was a dance hall known as the Plaza. It then became a bingo hall and is now a nightclub.

Competitors, all in fancy dress, line up for the Dongola Race at a regatta organised by engineering firm Drummond Bros on the River Wey, believed to be downstream from the Wood Bridge sometime before World War One.

An ideal way to finish an afternoon on the river was to enjoy a refreshing cuppa at Leroy's Tea Gardens at the boat house off the Shalford Road.

Are the figures in this picture contemplating a spot of rock climbing on the outcrop of greensand at St Catherine's? The hill with its chapel, built in the fourteenth century but a ruin since the sixteenth century, was for centuries the site of an annual fair. It has also been a place of recreation for scores of Guildfordians. Indeed, many people, young and old, have and still do clamber over parts of the exposed sand – and many a child's Sunday best clothes have been stained bright orange as a result.

The road at Newlands Corner looks rather narrow in this picture dating from the 1920s. Today, bushes and trees have partially obscured this view. The road up from Merrow over the Downs and on to Gomshall is, of course, still popular with weekend motorists enjoying the spectacular countryside.

When Guildford Golf Club was founded just over 100 years ago, this imposing house in Warren Road was the clubhouse. The inland links stretched out across Merrow Downs. Members in this 1893 illustration are standing closer to the position of the current clubhouse, completed in 1901. The man in black in the foreground is the Earl of Onslow, whose family had owned the Downs since coming to Clandon centuries before. Long before golfers had moved on to the wide open spaces, the Downs had been the venue of the annual Guildford Races, under the patronage of the Onslows, and with keen support from royalty. The meetings, on what was described as 'a fine circular course', were held every Whitsun week.

This lovely composition extolling the virtues of Guildford Golf Club appeared, it is believed, in the *London Illustrated News* in 1892.

Ladies on the putting green in 1902, with their caddies, a year after the opening of the present clubhouse at Merrow. Since leaving its first headquarters in Warren Road in the late 1890s, the club had been in premises at the top of High Path Road.

SURREY COUNTY HOSPITAL.

EXHIBITION MATCHES

will be played on the Links of the

GUILDFORD GOLF CLUB,

MERROW DOWNS,

ON

WEDNESDAY, 13th SEPTEMBER, 1922,

BY MESSRS.

BRAID, H. VARDON E. RAY & G. CAWKWELL

in the Morning and Afternoon on behalf of the

FUNDS OF THE HOSPITAL.

The whole of the Expenses will be met by Members of the Club.

Collections will be made on the Links to which all onlookers will be expected to contribute, and the whole of the sum so collected will go to the Hospital.

Mills & Sons, Printers, Ltd., Castle Street, Guildford.

The passage of time has not changed Guildford Golf Club's priorities when it comes to raising money for charity. In 1922, the Surrey County Hospital benefited from midweek exhibition matches played by some of the biggest names in the sport. Seventy-five years on and the club continues to support the district hospital and its many charities.

Guildford Chamber of Trade was founded in 1905 and enabled the business people of the town to carry out their own form of networking, Edwardian-style. Here, members compete in the annual bowls tournament in the Castle Grounds. The players were continuing a pastime and a sport which had been followed on the site since at least 1739, and is today enjoyed

by members of Castle Green Bowling Club, which is celebrating its 75th anniversary this year. The club has a copy of a map prepared in 1739 by Matthew Richardson of Guildford, accountant and surveyor, which showed a bowling green in the Castle Grounds, and there is a record of Alderman Frederick Augustine Crooke and his father before him having been tenants of the green for 100 years up to the 1880s.

No. 24.....

GUILDFORD CHAMBER of TRADE.

Excursion to Portsmouth.

WEDNESDAY, JULY 12TH, 1911.

TICKET 10/6 Including Saloon Carriages, Luncheon, Tea, &c.

Leave Guildford at 7.34.   Return from Portsmouth at 8.50.

B. E. HARDY,
W. TRIGGS TURNER, } *Hon. Secs.*

Traders, their wives and friends, 212 in all, in front of Portsmouth Town Hall on their annual summer outing on Wednesday, 12 July 1911. They were led by the Chamber of Trade president, Ernest Edgley, and enjoyed 12 hours by and on the sea. The large party travelled by train to Portsmouth and toured the city in trams before lunching at the Esplanade Hotel in Southsea. The steamboat *Duchess of Richmond* was boarded for a three-hour cruise in the Solent.

Day trip to Southsea: A party of Guildford residents arrive at the Esplanade Hotel in Southsea in the 1920s aboard a charabanc hired from Pearl Grey Coaches. The boy at the rear of the vehicle is Peter Pallot, Onslow Village born and bred and still living in Guildford's garden suburb.

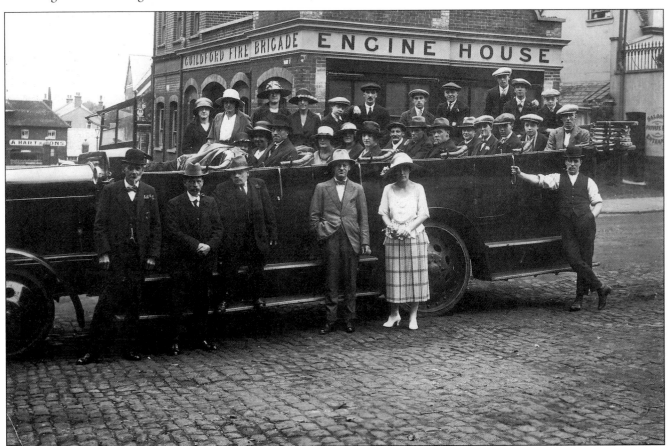

Off on another outing: A charabanc loaded with Guildford residents, also in the 1920s, waits to pull away from outside the fire station in North Street. Beyond the bonnet of the vehicle can be seen the Martyr Road horticultural business of A.Hart and Sons, now the site of the *Surrey Advertiser*.

Proud members of the Friary Brewery Silver Band pose for an official photograph in 1932. Judging by the trophies on display, the band contained a wealth of useful musicians. It is still in existence and regularly competes with the best of Britain's brass bands.

Hold it right there! The Mayor of Guildford, William Harvey, opens the Lido in 1933, watched by civic dignitaries and members of the public. Alderman Harvey was instrumental in the building of the Lido. His brainwave to help overcome the problem of unemployment in the town was the Work Fund of 1932, to which all residents of the borough were asked to contribute weekly until enough money was raised to keep 600 men employed. Money poured in, the Lido was built and Alderman Harvey was rewarded for his efforts by being appointed an OBE and an honorary freeman of the borough.

Some things never change, only the fashions of the swimsuits! On a hot summer's day Guildford Lido was as popular when it was first opened as it is today. Postcard publishers of the 1930s came in their droves to capture the scene. And in turn those cards were soon posted to friends and relatives with messages saying what a great time they had had splashing about in the pool. In the background you can just make out the Lido car park. Many of the motorists would have used the newly opened A3 to get there.

Aspidistras and glazed tiles all went to make up Guildford's indoor swimming pool – the Castle Street Baths. This 1920s photograph shows the attendants, including William Whitbourn, in the centre, who was in charge of the baths from 1913 to 1950.

The 186-acre Stoke Park was bought by the borough council in 1925 to safeguard it from development and opened to the public for recreation. Paths and gardens were created including a rockery with a paddling pool and boating lake on either side. The pool is shown here in the 1950s with the long-since demolished mansion in the background.

Henley Fort, situated on The Mount, was built in 1896. It once formed part of the western fortification of London. For the last 40 years it has been used as a camp and activity centre for young people. In the early days the accommodation was somewhat spartan, but in recent times the county council-run centre has been modernised and now the outdoor education centre contains information and displays recreating life in a Victorian fort.

Christopher Ede and now David Clarke have been pageant masters in Guildford for more than 40 years. These two photographs show scenes from the 1957 Pageant of Guildford in Shalford Park, in which Christopher Ede was the master and David Clarke the production designer.

In 1968, the Pageant of England drew large crowds, including J.Paul Getty and friends from his then home at Sutton Place, just outside Guildford, to Shalford Park. David Clarke was both pageant master and designer for this event which traced nearly 2,000 years of English history from Boudicca's rebellion in AD60 to World War One. It was the culmination of 18 months' work for Mr Clarke, who not only wrote the script but designed the costumes worn by the 1,000 actors and actresses. These photographs show (above) children assembled for a pre-production procession in the High Street and (below) the cavalcade of performers passing through the centre of the town.

Princess Anne, as royal patron, attended the Silver Jubilee Pageant in 1977 when David Clarke was again master and designer. Among the almost 3,000 performers, were these combatants who enacted a scene from the Civil War.

Loseley Park was the backdrop for *A Midsummer Night's Dream* in 1965. Here, David Clarke, as director/designer, and Bice Bellairs, the choreographer, conduct a rehearsal with girls who were in the fairy group. Miss Bellairs, who died in 1991, founded the Bellairs Studio of Dance and Drama in 1961 and, three years later, the acclaimed Guildford School of Acting and Dance.

It is summer, the exams are over and it is free festival time at the University of Surrey. Students and the public were invited on to the Stag Hill campus for its yearly arts festival which ran from the 1970s into the 1980s. Back in the 1970s it was a big event with rock bands playing on an outdoor stage. Films and other styles of music could be enjoyed inside and thousands of young people had a good time – even if the amplified sound of progressive rock could be heard as far away as Stoughton.

Football –
The Pinks & The City

Long before the much mourned Guildford City Football Club was formed, soccer supporters cheered on Guildford FC, known as the Pinks, an amateur club which was founded in 1877 and continued until 1953. The Pinks' first pitch was on a sports ground in Woodbridge Road, which later became the town's cattle market, and they are pictured there in 1895-96, their only season in the Southern League. Back row (left to right): Farrow, G.W.Scott, G.Baker, T.Arnold (goalkeeper), W.Bewsey, J.W.Jones. Front: G.S.Farnfield, A.J.Farnfield, A.S.Farnfield, F.Higlett, L.B.Rees.

The Pinks in the early part of this century when the captain (with the ball) was Dan Fere. On his right is L.C. 'Jack' Ede who later became a director of Guildford City FC.

In 1920-21, the Pinks, by then playing on the present Woodbridge Road sports ground, were champions of the Southern Suburban League. Back row (left to right): A.W.Balchin, E.Booth, W.H.C.Hobson, G.L.Russell, J.Barringer, S.H.Northcott, H.I.Blowfield. Middle: D.J.Stevens, A.Giles, A.A.Gowan, L.Byrne, T.Cooper, E.Bartlemeh, G.J.Reading, A.Grove, E.H.Carley, W.Titley. Front: W.A.Coote, A.Grove, A.E.Mills, W.Smith, L.C.Ede, R.L.Pearcy, L.Harrison, F.G.Chittleburgh. Steven Northcott, who taught at Pewley School until he retired in 1927, was a former goalkeeper with the club who went on to serve as chairman of Surrey County Football Association for some years.

The ground at Josephs Road in 1921, prior to Guildford United Football Club's first season. The grandstand, which seated 570 people, was designed by Frederick Hodgson and built by the Guildford firm of Tribe & Robinson, which used one half of a World War One aircraft hangar as the roof. Mr Hodgson, Darlington-born but a prominent Guildfordian from 1908 until his death in 1971, designed the layout of the ground. The contract for the work, in the sum of £1,400, went to Walter Hogsden, of Gosden Nurseries, Bramley, who employed a couple of Guildford labourers, Alfred Henry King, of Woking Road, and William Brooks, of Mangles Road. It was not all plain sailing, though, and Messrs Hogsden, King and Brooks met in Godalming Crown Court over a payment dispute. The club's first match in the Southern League was against Reading Reserves on 27 August 1921, when a crowd of 6,000 saw the Mayor, Alderman G.W.Franks, kick off and United win 2-0. A practice match the week before had attracted 3,000 spectators.

The first line-up for Guildford United, before the match with Reading Reserves on 27 August 1921. Back row (left to right): W.Tucker (trainer), who had been with the Pinks, Harrison, Cooper, Shaw, Unknown. Middle: Unknown, Brickwood, Grimsdell, Gowan, Phillips (12th man), A.Bullen (secretary). Front: Smith, Hemming, Hodson (captain), Searby, Thompson. United remained part of the club's name until the end of the 1926-27 season when it restyled itself Guildford City to coincide with the formation of the Guildford diocese.

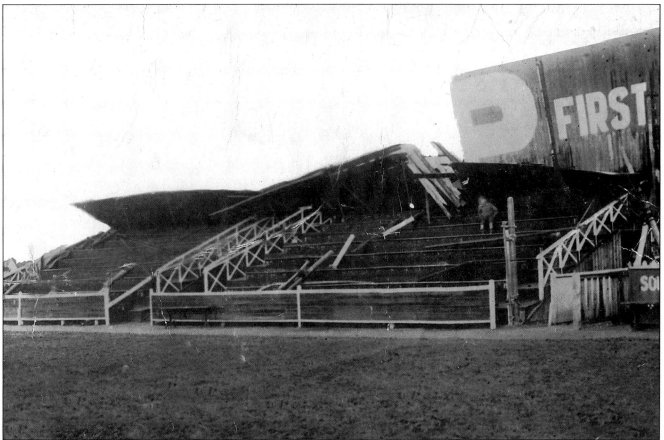

The professional football club suffered a big blow on the night of Friday, 6 December 1929, when the town was hit by gale force winds and torrential rain. The *Surrey Advertiser* reported on 14 December that one of the iron standards at the front, near the entrance to the dressing rooms, snapped, and two others were fractured, which caused the stand to lean 'some inches out of the perpendicular'. There was little danger of a collapse, but some amount of expense would be incurred in making it safe. After Christmas, the club made an appeal for £250 when its insurance company said the policy did not cover storm damage. It would cost £560 to rebuild the stand and bring the dressing rooms and other accommodation to its original state, but such a big scheme was not contemplated. However, dressing and bath accommodation had to be provided, and Robert Dickie, a director, said: 'If we could get £250, we could get on with the work.' While the repair work was being carried out, a neighbouring resident, Mr G.Hart, allowed his house, Parkfield, which stood on the north side of Josephs Road, at the Ladymead end, to be used as a dressing room. By the end of February, when City beat Poole 4-0, it was reported that the 'reconstructed main stand' was in use.

Guildford City in 1931. Back row (left to right): Andrew Wyllie (manager), Watson, Robinson, Oliver, Tucker (trainer). Middle: Rooke, Bailey, Ives, Polland, Davies. Front: Weale, Chappell, Maycock, Tinkler, Hyde. The star player was Ronnie Rooke, born at 2 Recreation Road, who went on to play for Arsenal and Fulham and won international honours.

Glory days. Guildford City's first Southern League title came in 1937-38 after an end-of-season run-in which saw the team head off Plymouth Argyle Reserves and Ipswich Town. Players were mobbed at the end of the final match and there was loud applause in the town's cinemas as the news was announced on the Saturday afternoon. The club celebrated with a dinner in the Royal Engineers' Hall. Back row (left to right): J.McFarlane, J.Todd, J.Hunter, Bill Ives, F.Over (trainer). Middle: Freddie Hodgson (who was a continuous director of the club, and several times chairman, from its inception until his death 50 years later), Arthur Grove, Jack Ede, Gerrard, Darvill, Willie Robb (the goalkeeper who had played for Rangers, Hibernian and Scotland in the 1920s), Jimmy Brown, Stan Denby, and directors Ingrey, W.A.Gammon, R.C.Jennings and A.Williams. Front: Hayden Green (manager), Bytheway, Johnny McPheat, Foulkes, Sammy Robinson, Dick Brown, Nelson Robinson, Charlie Barter (secretary). City won the league again in 1955-56.

A first round replay in the FA Cup against neighbours Aldershot on Wednesday, 30 November 1938, saw a record 9,989 spectators crammed into the Josephs Road ground. City lost 4-3 after a tremendous match which the Shots had led 3-0 before half-time. The cars and motorcycle combination are parked in Josephs Road. Immediately to the left of the telegraph pole is Woodbridge House, long since demolished, and on the extreme left is the power station which disappeared in the late 1960s.

Page three of the *Daily Mirror*, no less. The national newspaper no doubt had its eye on a one-day circulation boom in the home of the British Army after the Shots' pulsating FA Cup victory.

Big match programme when City played the Shots in the FA Cup replay at Josephs Road.

After the lean years of the war, during which German prisoners laid the concrete terracing at the Stocton Road end of the ground, Guildford City FC was back in business in 1946-47. Back row (left to right): Bill Lane (manager), Unknown, George Matthewson, Paddy Hennessy, Unknown, A.Anderson, Fred Over, Joe Todd (trainer). Front: Tommy Dougall, Ray Ellwood, Freddie Monk, Wilf Bott, Unknown.

Post-war action at Josephs Road with City defenders Anderson, Coulson and Matthewson watching a header from a Colchester United forward go safely into the arms of goalkeeper Paddy Hennessy (out of picture). City won 2-0 in front of a crowd of 4,132 with Maurice Roberts scoring both goals, one a penalty. The new supporters' club headquarters can be seen to the left of the main stand in this 1946-47 season shot.

City line up before the start of the 1947-48 season. The houses in Josephs Road and Stocton Road are in the background. Back row (left to right): Joe Todd, Walter Brine (groundsman), Mr Gordon, Peter Barton, George Matthewson, Paddy Hennessy, Bob Gunner, Ronnie Ranson, Freddie Hodgson, Arthur Williams. Front: Fred Bailey, Bill Lane (manager), A.Anderson, Tommy Dougall, Mr Hamilton Gordon (chairman), Freddie Monk, Maurice Kay, Fred Over (trainer), Charlie Barter (secretary). On ground: Reg Ellwood, Wilf Bott.

Another trophy for Guildford City, this time the Southern League Cup in 1966-67. It had previously won the competition in 1962-63. Back row (left to right): Freddie Hodgson, Unknown, Mac Sinclair, Les Brown, Danny Devine, Jack Fielding, Seth Vafiadis, Eric Gill, Sid Bishop, Phil Gunter, Peter Vasper, Bob Massey, Unknown, Peter Knight, Mr Cook (director), Albert Tennant (manager), Roy Baverstock (director). Front: Terry More, Tommy Anthony, Alan Gregory, Tony Burge, Darby Watts, Ray Colfar, Bill Golding (trainer).

Goalkeeper's ball. Slack, the flat-capped Cambridge United custodian, aided by a defender, stops Tony Burge during another attack in City's 3-1 win on 19 March 1966. This was Burge's second senior game, and he was soon established as a darling of the terraces.

Centre-forward Tony Burge wins this tussle in the Southern League match against Trowbridge on 12 December 1970. He scored once in a 5-2 win. After City folded, Burge remained involved in football locally until he died of cancer a few years ago. His son, Darren, who plays centre-half for Godalming and Guildford FC, has a scrapbook of his father's career, and we thank him for the loan of the photographs on this page.

The end is nigh. Supporters gather in the centre circle in 1974 to protest at the impending demise of Guildford City Football Club. The banner appears to carry the legend 'No to Dorking', a reference to the news that City was to merge with and play at Dorking. The two clubs came together briefly, but the death warrant for City had effectively been written. Fans heard on Friday, 15 February 1974, that the last match had been played at Josephs Road.

A picture to sadden the hearts of all football supporters. The winding up of Guildford City Football Club in 1974 left the Josephs Road ground looking like this in February 1975.

Fire swept through the main stand as arsonists attacked the ground in April 1974. The ground, which had been sold for £40,000 in 1970 to Guildford and Surrey Investments and was resold two years later to Joviel Properties Ltd for £200,000, was dug up and developed for housing in 1977 after it had been sold on to a housing association from Harrow. In the intervening years, there have been several unsuccessful attempts to revive the club although the supporters' club continues to be alive and kicking.

Special Events and Visits Making the News

An old ceremony known as Firing the Feux de Joir – firing gunpowder off the tops of anvils – is taking place at the Guildford Iron Foundry at Church Acre behind St Saviour's Church at the time of the Coronation of George V in 1911. Some of these buildings still survive and are now part of the Bellerby Theatre, named after Bill Bellerby who, with his wife Doreen, have been leading lights in the life of the town for more than 40 years. They were appointed MBE in a dual ceremony in 1991 and four years later were given the freedom of the borough.

Room for one more! An assorted band of Guildfordians, including a policeman, are standing in a barge waiting to cross the River Wey at St Catherine's while beating the bounds on 27 September 1905. The party would have walked the circumference of the borough (smaller than it is today) striking landmarks en route with sticks. Although an ancient custom, it seems that it was only revived in Guildford towards the end of the nineteenth century.

The Edwardian photographer records another procession down the High Street. The behatted ladies, and the gentlemen, too, for that matter, form part of a Congregational Church parade.

Hundreds of townspeople turned out as the funeral procession of Dr Francis Rutherford Russell passed down the High Street on 15 May 1908. The *Surrey Advertiser* reported that 'all day the town had borne an outward appearance of mourning' with flags at half-mast and shutters drawn. The funeral service was held at St Saviour's Church, where Dr Russell had been a sidesman, and the coffin was then carried by train to Edinburgh for burial. Dr Russell, 55, was a Scot who had moved to Guildford in 1882 to join the practice of Dr Sells, the founder of Charlotteville. He was prominent in the Volunteer movement and active in many organisations in the town. His hobby was engineering and in 1902 he helped to establish the firm of Drummond's at Rydes Hill. With the brothers Frank and Arthur Drummond, Dr Russell steered the company in such a way that at the time of his death, when he was chairman of the board, the staff had grown to 156. He had also been chairman of the Guildford Electricity Supply Company since 1897.

On 21 July 1908, the founder of the Salvation Army, General William Booth, while on a national tour, paid a visit to Guildford. A large crowd flocked to North Street to see the striking figure of the man with the long white beard as he arrived in a smart motor car.

The publicity machine of the women's suffragette movement of the early years of the twentieth century included this horse-drawn trailer which pulls no punches over the aims to get women in Britain the right to vote. Although the exact location is unknown, this photograph was published on a Guildford postcard. The young boys on the right were probably more interested in the photographer and his bulky equipment than the van itself.

This is the Charlotteville Cycling Club's float parading along North Street in the procession marking George V's Coronation on 22 June 1911. It was called The Rosary Walk, though from a distance the riders could be mistaken for French onion sellers! The cycle club was formed after men from Charlotteville met at the institute in Addison Road on 27 March 1903. Racing has featured prominently throughout the club's history. Indeed, there was a 25-mile time trial at the club's first event in 1905. The club is still very active today and organises the town centre cycle races each year as part of the Guildford Festival.

The Cornmarket in the High Street decorated for the Coronation of George V in 1911. It stands on the site of The Tuns Inn which was demolished along with an old wooden roofed cornmarket in 1818. Although the origins of the story are not known, it is said that in the last century there was a man who announced that he could carry a large sack of corn on his shoulders and walk all the way from Guildford to Farnham across the Hog's Back without stopping. He arrived, winning several bets in the process. He then decided to walk back again, but this time no one was willing to bet against him. Nevertheless, so the story goes, he walked back with the sack of corn anyway. The cornmarket closed in 1901 when business transferred to Woodbridge Road and the two central columns were moved in 1933 to allow vehicles to pass through the arch.

Gateway into Guildford: Among the celebrations for the Coronation of George V in 1911 was this handsome wooden arch erected at the foot of the High Street just before the Town Bridge. It butted up to St Nicolas Church on the right and The Connaught Hotel on the left.

A carnival procession makes its way up Markenfield Road towards Stoke Road in the 1920s. One of the vehicles belongs to Pitcher & Co, a local caterer.

This strangely 'doctored' photograph shows the visit by the then Duke and Duchess of York, later King George VI and Queen Elizabeth, to Guildford in April 1924 to open a new outpatients' wing at the Royal Surrey County Hospital in Farnham Road. The royal couple are greeted by, from left, the town clerk, Mr R.C.Knight, Alderman Rapkins, Alderman Baker (shaking hands with the duchess), Alderman Fentum Phillips and Alderman G.W.Franks.

The Rotary Club of Guildford was formed in 1921, 16 years after the movement was started by a Chicago businessman, Paul Harris. The club was the 50th to be established in Great Britain and Ireland. This photograph, taken in September 1924, shows three of its founder members at a presentation of the Stars and Stripes in Brett's Restaurant in Guildford. The flag was handed over by Pirie Macdonald, on behalf of the Rotary Club of New York. On the right is the Mayor of Guildford, Alderman H.E.Smith, JP, and next to him is Albert Hickling, a prime mover in

bringing the service organisation to the town and the president in 1925-26. Third from the left is William Massey, president in 1923. The president in 1924 was Mr L.C.Biddle.

More than three dozen of Guildford's leading businessmen of the 1950s are shown in this photograph taken at the rear of the Prince of Wales public house in Woodbridge Road. The occasion was a Round Table gathering. The two men seated wearing badges of office are Dick Hardy (left) and Austin Williams, beside whom is John Boyce, twice Mayor of Guildford. Seated on the far right is his brother, Ken, who, with his wife, took over the licence of the Prince of Wales from his parents after World War Two. The pub, which was demolished in 1972, had been in the Boyce family since 1881 when Ken's grandfather had taken over the management.

The day Our Gracie came to Guildford: Gracie Fields brightened the gloom of a post-war Dennis factory and is pictured with, on her right, her manager, Mr W.Bleach, and, on her left, Shaun McAlister, the compere of the show the star put on for the workers. Also photographed are Cecil T.Skipper (far left) and William Fish, who had been joint managing directors of Dennis Bros Ltd since 1942.

It is carnival time in 1935 and the float of Guildford City Football Club is passing along Stoke Road. The premises of T.Swayne & Son, long-standing building contractors, can be seen beyond the model of a City footballer.

To celebrate the jubilee celebrations of King George V on Monday, 6 May 1935, a temporary medieval-style arch, similar to the one in 1911, was constructed out of wood by the Town Bridge at the bottom of the High Street. It was a gloriously sunny day and the huge crowds which attended the many activities around the town voted it by far the best civic occasion they had witnessed.

God Save the King: Townspeople watch as the High Sheriff of Surrey, Sir Laurence Halsey, reads the proclamation of King Edward VIII on the steps of Holy Trinity Church in the High Street on Saturday, 25 January 1936. On his right is the Mayor of Guildford, Lawrence Powell, and behind is the chairman of Surrey County Council, Alderman J.Chuter Ede. The monarch, of course, did not remain on the throne very long, and the official business of proclaiming a new head of state was repeated the following year when Edward's brother became King George VI.

A delightfully informal shot taken on 1 April 1937, when Queen Mary visited Guildford to open the new maternity home, clinic and hostel of the Guildford Queen's District Nursing Association in Stoughton Road, which became known as the Jarvis Clinic. In the front row, from left, are Lt Col E.R.P.Berryman; Lady Jarvis; Miss Edwards, assistant superintendent; Mrs Bowyer; Miss Campion, superintendent; Queen Mary; Sir John Jarvis; Lt Col F.Ingram Ford; Mrs Doveton; Mr J.Garnett Harper, secretary of the Guildford branch of the Nursing Association; and Mr E.Stevens, treasurer of the Guildford branch. Members of staff are pictured behind. Sir John Jarvis, who was the MP for Guildford from 1934-50 and the High Sheriff in 1934-35, appealed through the *Surrey Advertiser* for the public to raise £16,600 to build the home, to which he and Lady Jarvis gave £4,000. The dairy firm Cow & Gate paid for the maternity unit. The home was opened by Queen Mary with a golden key which she then presented to Lady Jarvis. Nationally, Sir John, who died in October 1950, was known for his support for the unemployed on Tyneside. He founded five companies in Jarrow, which created 5,000 jobs, and was given the freedom of that borough.

A fine pair of boots, my lad! On Saturday afternoon, 15 July 1939, the then War Secretary, Leslie Hore-Belisha, visited Stoughton Barracks. The reason for his visit, according to the notes scribbled on the back of the original photograph, was to inspect the kit of the militiamen. Three years earlier, as Transport Minister, he had opened the Guildford bypass.

King George VI visited Stoughton Barracks in September and October 1939 to inspect the troops stationed there. As war broke out, the barracks became a training camp for many different types of army personnel. However, the cap badges of these commanders identifies them as from the Queen's Regiment.

It would seem that not only did the King meet the soldiers, but was also introduced to their wives as well. A curly-haired youngster gazes on in wonder.

Curiously, part of the King's visit to the barracks took place in the adjoining Stoughton Junior School. Here a Bren gun is demonstrated. The back of the original picture is stamped 'Ministry of Information Press Section' and was passed for publication on 25 October 1939. Note that all the men, including the King, of course, are carrying gas mask cases.

The High Sheriff of Surrey, Maj F.Paget-Hett, reads the Proclamation of Queen Elizabeth II on the steps of Holy Trinity Church, on Friday, 8 February 1952, two days after the nation had been stunned by the death of her father, King George VI. The *Surrey Advertiser* reported that for the first time in their lives thousands of people who jammed the High Street sang 'God save the Queen', many stumbling over the unfamiliar phrase. The town mourned the death of a well-loved monarch with church services and acts of remembrance at meetings and sporting events.

To mark the 700th anniversary of the granting of the first Charter to the Borough of Guildford by Henry III, the Queen and Prince Philip spent a busy day in the town on Thursday, 27 June 1957. Travelling by car from Sandhurst, the royal couple was welcomed by the Mayor, Alderman Harold Kimber, at the Guildhall. From there they visited the cathedral, the Royal Surrey County Hospital, spent some time at Shalford Park watching the finale of the Pageant of Guildford, and ended the day at the Woodbridge Road sports ground where Surrey beat Hampshire by an innings and 73 runs.

The weather on the day of the Queen's visit was glorious. The *Advertiser* reported that it was 'a day when the golden June sunshine picked out the gaily festooned streets; the Union Jacks and streamers clutched in the hands of excited children, the summer dresses and the shirt-sleeved men'. Crowds lined the town's streets wherever the royal pair went. In fact, they were due to see some of the cricket at Woodbridge Road, but when they arrived late in the afternoon the match had finished. However, while the Queen enjoyed a strawberry tea, the two teams played a hastily arranged 20-over match.

The Guildford tradition of presenting a monarch with a plum cake on a visit to the town was carried out on the balcony of the Guildhall. As a reigning monarch had not made an official visit to the town for 300 years, some research had to be done to find a suitable recipe. The Guildford Master Bakers' Association helped out and a fruit cake was baked at a Guildford bakery by young apprentices under expert supervision. Here, the Queen receives the cake from the High Steward, Lord Onslow. Also pictured, from the left, are the MP for Guildford, Richard Nugent

(later to become Lord Nugent and a freeman of the borough), the Recorder, Mr T.Christmas Humphreys, the Mayor, Alderman Harold Kimber, and the town clerk, H.C. 'Sam' Weller.

Matthew and Catherine Howse, aged seven and nine respectively, pictured in the High Street decorated for the Queen's Silver Jubilee during the summer of 1977. Street parties, fetes and shows were held across the borough and a beacon was lit on The Mount on Sunday, 7 June. The Guildford beacon should have been lit directly after the one at Windsor. However, strict timekeeping by the Royal Institute of Chartered Surveyors, which had organised the nationwide bonfire network, prompted the Lord Lieutenant, Lord Hamilton of Dalzell, to light the Guildford fire at the arranged time of 10.03pm. This was in fact seven minutes before the Queen lit the Windsor beacon.

Dicing for the Maid's Money is an age-old tradition held each year at the Guildhall. It forms part of the annual meeting of the trustees of the Guildford Municipal Charities. The money for the dicing custom comes from two charities formed by Guildfordians John How and John Parsons, in 1674 and 1702 respectively. Originally open to serving maids in the town, in recent years the organisers have found it difficult to attract applicants. Now single women working in private houses in the borough for at least five days a week are eligible. The loser always wins, taking the Parsons charity money, now about £62, a couple of pounds more than the How charity which goes to the winner. Pictured at the 1966 contest are Doris Lazenby and Mabel Randle.

A close-up view of the huge crowd that packed the High Street to greet Princess Anne on her visit to Guildford on the afternoon of Wednesday, 6 July 1977. The princess, who was expecting her first child, Zara, later that year, had a busy day, also visiting Wisley Gardens and elderly people in Effingham. At Guildford, she went to Abbot's Hospital, the Guildhall, saw a Queen's Silver Jubilee exhibition at Guildford House and attended a performance of the pageant at Shalford Park in the evening. Massive security was in operation with more than 100 police officers involved from three divisions, including Special Branch, with a reserve squad on stand-by.

Subscribers

J.M.Adams
William Airey
Mr John W.Allford
Raymond A.Amos
Bob Archer
Catherine Armitage
Mrs Marjory Arnold
Rev & Mrs Fredrik Arvidsson
Kate Askew
Derek J.Atkinson
Don Avery
Joan Bailey-Lienard
Mr J.Baker
Joan Ball
Ivy Bampton
John Band
Mrs P.M.Barnett
Nicholas Bateman
B.J.Bateson
Mrs M.Batty
A.R.C.Beisley
C.J.C.Bell
Mr C.Bellchambers
Bill Bellerby
Manuel Bello-Gomez
Joan Benge (née Bullen)
A.Bicknell
John Black
Mrs E.Blackwood
R.F.Blake
Charles Boardman
Mrs Sheila Boddy
William Bolton
Mr D.Bond
E.Bond
Margaret Bookham
Arthur Bovingdon
Anne & Les Bowerman
Ray M.Bowes
Jack Boxall
L.R.Boxall
Barbara J.Boyce
Mr & Mrs G.Breckell
N.H.Briggs
Mrs T.M.Briggs
A.J.F.Brown
David F.Brown
J.F.Brown
Mrs Mollie Brown
P.J.F.Brown
Peter D.Bullen
Muriel Bullingham
R.H.Bullock
Miss M.Burdett
Nickolas Burfield
R.G.K.Burgess
Mr M.Burke
T.Burnard
Shirley Burrill
Lorna Marie Burrows
Mrs O.J.Burton
Mrs Sue Bushell
Edward Bye

Ernest Caffell
Ian Cakebread
Russell Carr
Frank Carter
Ian Carter
Anna M.Cartwright
Jeremy D.Cartwright
Rodney Y.Cartwright
Samantha May Cast
Mr & Mrs R.G.Chalcraft
Joan Chandler
Christopher Cheesman
Kevin J.Chesson
Mr & Mrs A.Chudley
Roy Chudley
Clare's Pantry, Bramley
Muriel Clark
Marjorie Clifford
Mrs S.M.Codling
W.J.Comley
Lesley Connor
Mrs M.J.Cooper
John Corrie
Dorothy Court
Florence Coyne
The Crittendons
Miss M.E.Crooke
R.H.Crowcombe
Tony Crowley
Mr & Mrs H.Cunningham
Jane Currie
Sheila Anne Cuthbert
S.N.Das
Janis Day
Mr N.J.Deacon
Michael Dean
W.P.Dean
Stephen & Peter Denly
Mrs Dorothy Dodd
Mrs E.Donald
Elizabeth Douglas
J.S.Downham
Tim Downing
Eileen Drummond
D.H.Durrant
Ivan Earle
Margaret Earle
D.T.Eason
Donald Edwards
Julie & Michael Edwards
Mollie Edwards
Mr & Mrs T.R.Edwards
Dudley Ekberg
D.Eley & E.Williams
Evelyn Elliott
E.Ellis
Julian Ellis
Peter Elsing
Edward John Elson
Chris & Grania Elston
Mary Elton
Mr J.T.Evans
R.C.Evans

Mrs Christine Everard
Jennifer Rose-Louise Everest
John Fairclough
Mrs Pamela Ferguson
Mr & Mrs A.Fielden
Jack Fielden
D.M.Fisher
Trevor Fisher
Des Flanders
Richard Ford
John Fowler
Mrs Linda Fowler (née Sankey)
P.R.Fowler
Alison Francis
Douglas F.Francis
M.H.Freeman
Ann & Eric Fuller
F.J.Furlonger
Mrs H.M.J.Gafford
Arthur Edward Gale
Masie Gamelin
Richard & Niki Gan
B.D.Garbutt
S.A.Garnett
Jason Gibbons
Phyllis M.Gocher
Hilary & Jon Goff
Alan Goldsworthy
Alvina Gould
Katharine Graham
Richard Green
Kevin Greenhill
Roy Grey
Imogen Grieves
Mrs Mary Griffin (née Marrable)
Mr & Mrs A.Grimshaw
John & Jan Grindel
Audrey Grisdale
David Gumbrell
Alan Ronald Gunner
Ronald Gunner
Mr Brian Habgood
Brian Hailstone
Mr & Mrs A.C.Hall
Mary J.Hall (née Diplock)
Nicholas Robert Hall
Stuart James Hall
Ellen & Mark Hallam
Sheila Hallett
J.Halstead
Mrs C.M.Hammond
Mr W.J.Harding
Mr D.Harris
H.G.Harris
John & Sheila Harris
June M.Harris
Ann & Peter Harrison
Stephen Hatcher
Jean Hays
Audrey Head
Mr G.J.Healy
Sally Hedgecoe
Valerie Helliwell

Grace Hemming
Mr Andrew Henwood
Mrs V.A.Hickford
Mr Arthur Royston Hill
Brenda Hill
Mary M.Hill
Mr A.Hitchcock
Mr & Mrs N.Hodges
John Hodgson ARIBA
Mrs Joyce Hodgson
Mr G.Hofner
Graham Hoile
Mr A.V.Holbrook
Jake Andrew Holding
Pam Holmes
D.S.Hooke
O.F.Hopley
Anita Horne
Mrs Diana Hough (née Harris)
Mrs Judy Houghton
Mrs M.Howard
R.Howard
Dennis H.Howes
Vic Hudson
John Huggins
Mrs M.A.Hunt
L.J. & E.Hurlow
Mrs F.A.Hutchins
Mrs G.C.Jackson
Mrs T.Janes
Mr G.R.Jay
Peter Jenkinson
Johnson-Foxbury
J.Johnson
Michael M.Johnson
Mr John M.Keane
Valerie Ann Kelly
Wendy Kings
Terence Knight
Mrs M. de Kretser
Christina Lambley
Ian Lane
Sue & Derek Langridge
E.G.Lass
Mrs Margaret Lasseter
Aunt Laurel in Australia
Bruce Lawrence
E.G. & V.C.B.Lawrence
Kim Susan Lawrence
T.H.D.Lawrence
Julia & Paul Lindford-Relph
Mrs B.J.Lochead
Annie Lovell
Mr & Mrs Luck
Mr W.J.McCoy
Miriam Macdonald
Jacquelyn Rita McLeod
Mr David Maddox
N.F.Martin
G.T.Matthews
Robert James Matthews
S.Matthews
Bob Meaney
M.J.Merritt
Shirley Mewes
David F.J.Middleton
Patrick J.Millar
Ted Mills
Mrs M.Mitchell
Mrs P.M.Montgomery
Richard Mooney
Eric S.Morgan
Carole Ann Morley

Nathan Morley
Peter A.Morley
Mrs Jean Morris
Phyl & John Morris
Mr E.Moseling
J.M.Mount
G.W.Murphy
Mrs J.Nash
Stuart Neilson
Stanley Newman
Roger & Jennifer Nicholas
Barrie Alan Nurse
Muriel Olson
Arthur W.J.G.Ord-Hume
Colin Osborne
Mrs Dawn Page
D.H.P.Panton
Joyce Paramour
Charles Parker
H.J.Parker
Katherine Lauren Parker
Ron Parnell, Happy 80th Birthday
T.E.Parvin
D.W.Passells
Alderman J.B.Patrick & Mrs Enid Patrick (former
    Mayor, 1985-86)
Terence & Angela Patrick
Julia Pavia
Mr & Mrs R.R.Pawley
Doris Peck
G.E.Perkins
Mr G.A.M.Peters
John Watling Pettett
Mrs A.E.Pierce
Eileen Pierce
Mrs Mollie Pigdon
Mrs Daphne Pillar
Margaret Potter
Mrs N.Povey
Doreen Powell
Ruby L.Powell
D.H.Price
Mr & Mrs J.A.Price
Maureen Mary Proffitt
M.B.Prudence
Mrs J.Purkiss
Dr S.Quick
Mrs P.D.Quigley
Allan C.Read
Joan Read
Mrs Pauline Read
Mr & Mrs R.M.Read
Mr B.L.Reeves
Mr Ian Rice
Erica Richards (neé Harris)
Mary E.Riddle
Alan Riddy
Beryl Joyce Ritz
David Roberts
David Robins
Mrs S.Robinson
Sonja D.Robinson
Josephine & Denis Rooke
Robin B.Rose
A.P.Rossides
David Ryder
Margaret & John Saunders
Chris Seward
D.A.Seymour
Mrs Jean Rosemary Shaw
Mr A.Sherwin
Mr A.J.Simmonds
Mr Norman G.Simmonds

Elizabeth Skegg
Peter Slade
Leonard Smart
David Smith
David & Linda Smith
Graham Smith
Jane Smith
John Smith
John & Eve Smith
Kay & Ron Smith
Mr Paul Smith
Robert & Mary Smith
Mrs Sylvia Somner
Mr R.Standing
Chris Stanton
Mrs J.Stevens
Michael Roy Stevens
Tom & Sheila Stewart
Mrs P.Stokes
Heather Sheila Stone
Wendy Stone
Mr & Mrs L.Stratford
Derek John Street
Derek & Sheila Strugnell
Phyllis Stuart
Mr R.P.Style
James Sutherland
John C.Sutton
L.W.Tallant
Mrs Joyce Tate
Geoffrey Taylor
Jean & Alan Tedder
Anna Thomas
Janice Townley (née Ellis)
Mr & Mrs J.Trickey
Peter R.Turner
David Richard Tye
Takako Uchida
Gillian Vinall
H.Vincent
Mrs Jeanette Wakeford
John Wakely
David Walker
Pat Walker
Barney J.Wallace
Mrs Ethel Wallis
Tracey & Gary Wallis
Mark Watmough
Don Watts
In Memory of Bill Webb
Ivor Webster
J.Wells
Maureen & Ken Wells
Brian Wenman
Phyllis Wheeler
Joan Whitham
Roy & Ann Wigmore
Vera Wilkinson
Trevor & Christine Wilks
Austin Williams
Mrs J.F.Williamson
Peter Williamson
Mr & Mrs J.Winterton
David Wood
Thomas Woodger
Mr P.Wright
Eric Wye
Mr K.Yeates